CUSTOM Dressing Dolls

Helen B. Hanson

ISBN 0-943470-17-X

Introduction

All my life I have enjoyed sewing. For over twenty-five years many ladies, both young and old, have been in contests, gone to parties, danced at dances and participated in weddings wearing gowns of my creation.

They came to me with pictures to copy, sometimes with an idea of their own from which I created a gown, but most often for a custom-made gown of my own design.

Eventually after retiring, I discovered the joy of porcelain doll making and transferred my love of dressing beautiful girls to dressing beautiful dolls.

Had anyone told me a few years ago that I would be writing a book on dressing dolls my comment would have been "No way!"

Since then I have learned not to make predictions, because when you do dolls, one thing can lead to another, and I found that as others saw my dolls and their clothing, I had many requests to give lessons. I also found that giving lessons was very time consuming, and I was unable to reach everyone who wanted help. So the comment "No way!" has become a show and tell book on "My way."

There probably are other methods that are better or easier, but the world of doll costuming can give a person much enjoyment and satisfaction — especially if you know how to transfer your ideas to your dolls and have the results please you.

For good results of original designs, first visualize your idea in your mind's eye. Then, with the information given in this book, you should be able to transfer them to your doll, or use a commercial doll pattern and embellish it with your ideas.

This book was written for the beginner as well as the creative, advanced doll costumer.

One chapter has information on cloth bodies. Another tells how to make and fit a basic pant pattern, from which everything — from skimpy panties to a male doll's tuxedo pants can be made.

Trimmings constitute one chapter covering buttons to elaborate braid trims. Self trims, ribbon and cloth flowers and laces are also featured in this chapter, along with other trims.

Information about shoes, bonnets, hats, underclothing, dresses, coats and other things is given as I said before "my way." If your way works better for you, that's fine, but all I can do is show and tell my way, and if I help you, then the time and effort expended in preparing this book will have been worthwhile.

It is my wish, through text and pictures, to explain my methods in an understandable way, and if you have any questions, please feel free to write to me in care of Daisy Publications.

Sincerely,

Helen B. Hansen

Contents

Acknowledgements

Thanks to Judy Anderson for reading the book for understandability and proofreading the completed text.

Thanks to Laura Edgar for her excellent work in typing the manuscript.

Thanks to Marvin L. Hansen for the fine step-by-step pictures and small photos featured throughout the book.

Thanks to Mark Hains, master photographer, for the large photos of my dolls.

Thanks to Ed and Judy Anderson for permission to feature the dolls they have sculpted and dressed.

Thanks to Randy and Diane Martindale for using some of their dolls.

Any other acknowledgment will accompany the pictures used.

Last and very important, I wish to pay tribute with love to my understanding husband whose many acts of kindness and words of encouragement helped to make the compiling of this book much easier.

Dedication

"I dedicate this book to the Dolls' in my life, including fifteen beautiful grandchildren, who have given us much joy, a delightful trio of great-grandchildren, and the many fascinating life-like dolls that have made this book possible."

Forward

Please, before starting any garment, read the complete book and then read again that chapter pertaining to what you are making before starting because even though all of this is clear in my mind, I may not have conveyed my ideas to you as clearly as I wished. Also, I have, in a place or two, left some instructions for you to figure out, but there is enough basic information that you should be able to do that without any problems.

Always remember that the pattern making method given here is without seams, and a seam allowance must always be added to the pattern where needed.

I usually use ¼" seams. On some garments, a little larger seam allowance at the waistline and the closings is allowed.

A good paper to use when pinning a pattern to the doll for fitting purposes is a soft, strong paper towel. If you use a commercial doll clothing pattern, cut it first in paper towelling and fit it to your doll because it may need to be adjusted for a more sloping shoulder, or a shorter or deeper armeye, or a lower neckline, or some other fitting problem. This is better corrected in paper than in the fabric of the garment.

If the doll clothing is to be played with by children and the dolls dressed and undressed many times, I suggest that good washable material be used and all of the fasteners and buttons be sewn on securely. It is wise to use durable trims and keep the lines simple. Sew all of the seams by machine or carefully by hand without leaving any raw places to fray.

Sometimes for small children, it's best to have the doll's garments open flat for easy dressing.

However, when dressing the beautiful showy dolls that may last into antiquity, do the very best you possibly can making lovely tucks and ruffles, using yards of ribbon and laces and the most beautiful trims you can make or find. Because, not only will you take great pleasure in an exciting accomplishment, but at some future date, that beautiful costume with its fine workmanship will be a choice piece of memorabilia and a wonderful heritage.

I hope you will enjoy and profit from using this book.

Sincerely,
Helen

Glossary

AFGHAN — A soft coverlet, knitted or crocheted in a pattern.

ANTIQUE — Of an earlier period.

APPLIQUE — One type or piece of material applied to another, usually with needlework.

ARMSEYE — Same as armhole in a garment.

BASTE — To sew loosely together with temporary stitches.

BATISTE — A fine cotton fabric in plain weave named after a French weaver.

BATT — A wadded cotton or wool prepared in sheets or rolls.

BATTING — Same as batt.

BONDED BATTING — Batting held together with a substance to prevent looseness.

BEADING — (1) To sew beads to an article.
(2) A narrow open work through which ribbon can be run.

BIAS — A line running obliquely across the fabric on an angle to the horizontal and vertical weaves.

BINDING — (1) To enclose and provide with a border for decoration.
(2) To sew or otherwise bring two seams together.

BODICE — The upper portion of a garment.

BOUFFANT — A full skirt.

BOX-PLEAT — A pleat with the folds meeting towards each other.

BRAID — (1) To weave together several strands.
(2) A narrow flat tape for ornamenting garments.

BRIM — The projecting rim of a hat.

BROCADE — A rich fabric interwoven with a raised design.

BUNTING — A type of wrap or sleeping bag for baby dolls.

BUTTONHOLE TWIST — A special silk thread on bobbin-type wooden spools used for handmade buttonholes on heavier fabrics.

CASING — A covering.

CATCH-BY-HAND — To sew by hand securing the fabric in one place.

CHEMISE — A loose undergarment resembling a short slip.

CHIFFON — A sheer rayon or silk fabric; also can be made of polyester.

CLIP — (1) To cut in from outside edge to the stitch.
(2) To cut off excess material.

CORD — Several strands twisted together and used as ties or decoration on garments.

CORDING — A yarn or string enclosed in a bias strip and used for trim in seams.

CORDUROY — A fabric with raised velveteen-like lines.

CREASE — To fold on a line and usually pressed to hold.

CREPE — A thin fabric with a crinkled surface.

CREPE-DE-CHINE — A soft silk fabric with a pebbly surface.

CRINOLINE — (1) A stiff fabric with lots of sizing.
(2) A petticoat worn sometimes with hoops to hold out a full dress.

CROCHET — To form a lace with thread and a hook.

DART — A tapering tuck.

DOTTED SWISS — A sheer, crisp cotton fabric with woven dots.

DOWEL — A round wooden stick.

DRESS — (1) To put on garments.
(2) An outer garment.

ELASTIC — A thread-covered rubber to be used in sewing.

EMBROIDERY — To stitch a design on fabric with thread or yarn.

ENGLISH NET — A small-hole, cotton net. It can be made of silk for lace backing.

EYELET — A fabric with embroidered holes in a pattern or an edging with embroidered holes.

FABRIC — Materials from which clothing is constructed.

FACING — A partial lining turned back.

FLOSS — An embroidery thread.

FLUTING — A shaped flare.

FLY — The front opening of trousers.

FLY-SIMULATED — A false fly made with stitches.

GABARDINE — A firm twilled fabric with a raised diagonal weave.

GALLOON — A braid or lace with border on both sides, usually not very wide.

GARMENT — Clothing.

GEORGETTE — A sheer dull fabric with a crepe surface.

GORES — A triangular or tapering section in garments.

GOWN — (1) A loose night dress.
(2) A formal dress.

GRAIN — The woven lines in fabric.

HEM — An edge finished by turning the raw edge under and stitching.

HORSEHAIR BRAID — A bias braid of loosely woven synthetic strands used for hats, hems, etc. A stiff braid.

HORSEHAIR CLOTH — A cloth interwoven with actual horsehair used for innerlining in suits.

INNERLINING — Any fabric used to reinforce between the fabric and lining.

INSERTION — A strip of lace sewn between two pieces of fabric.

JOINT — A section on the cloth body of a doll that allows bending.

JOINING — That area where things are joined or the bringing together of two or more things.

KNOT — The tying section of a bow or an intertwining of ribbon to form an ornament.

LACE — (1) To thread ribbon or cord through holes.
(2) A fabric with delicate openwork on net.
(3) A narrow dainty fabric used for decoration on garments.

LAP — To lay one piece over the other, usually just over the edge.

LINEN — A fabric made from flax.

LINED — To make a garment that fits inside of another garment to cover the seams.

LINES — The shape or style of a garment.

LOOPS — An extension of thread or other materials to assist in closing a garment. Decorative holes made with ribbon or other materials by folding and bringing one end to the other.

MARK — To designate the place with a pencil, chalk, thread, pins or any other method.

MATERIAL — Cloth or fabric.

MUSLIN — A plain weave cotton fabric.

NAP — The short fibers forming a downy or fuzzy surface on fabric.

NET — A fabric woven with an open pattern.

NOTCH — To make a mark either by cutting out a section of fabric or extending a small V of fabric for matching purpose.

ORGANDY — A thin transparent fabric made of cotton, silk or synthetic fibers.

OVERCASTING — To completely or partially cover a raw edge with thread by hand or machine.

PANEL — One or more pieces of fabric sewn lengthwise in a garment.

PANTALOONS — A tight fitting undergarment for hips and legs, worn under crinolines.

PARASOL — An umbrella-shaped sun shade.

PERCALE — A closely woven cotton fabric without gloss.

PICOT — The loop on a lace edge or a crochet knot on the edge of crocheting.

PIECE — To add on material for size.

PINCH — To hold tightly between two fingers.

PLACKET — An opening in a garment to enable it to be put on. Can be made by allowing enough fabric to be folded back or by adding a separate piece and sewing it on as a binding.

PLEAT — A fold in the fabric to create fullness, usually pressed flat.

PRINCESS CUT — A fitted garment cut in gores without a cut waistline.

QUILT — A covering for a bed.

QUILTING — The art of sewing together two fabrics with padding between, usually hand sewn.

RAVEL — To separate threads or fibers.

RIBBON — A narrow piece of silk or other fabric with finished edges and made in various weaves.

ROSETTE — A flower-like ornament made of various materials, used for decorations.

RUFFLE — A gathered piece of fabric, lace or ribbon.

SATIN — A fabric of silk or synthetic fibers of thick texture, usually having a glossy side and a dull side.

SATEEN — A cotton satin.

SELVAGE — The edge of a woven fabric.

SELVADGE — The edge of a woven fabric.

STRAND — A length of fiber or fibers.

TAFFETA — A fine woven, somewhat stiff fabric of silk or other fibers.

TAPE — A variety of narrow materials, some with finished edges — as twill tape, and some cut on the bias.

TASSEL — A dangling ornament consisting of loose hanging threads or cords.

THREAD — (1) A slender cord of two or more strands of cotton or other fibers and used in needlework.
(2) To lace through beading or other open spaces.

TRICOT — A fine knitted medium weight material. Can also be sheer.

TUBE — Cloth arm and leg parts that are sewn together to make a cylinder.

TUCK — A folded piece of material in a garment, usually sewn.

SIMULATED TUCK — A machine stitch resembling a tiny tuck used for decoration.

TULLE — A fine stiff net.

ULTRA SUEDE — An imitation leather that comes in many colors and is expensive.

UNRAVEL — To separate threads or fibers.

VEILING — A fine soft net used for bridal veils.

VELOUR — A fabric resembling velvet, usually with a knitted back.

VELVET — A rich fabric with a thick pile on one side made of silk or synthetic fibers.

VELVETEEN — A cotton velvet.

VOILE — A fine sheer fabric.

WHIP STITCH — A hand stitch that joins with a close even stitch.

YARN — Continous thread-like material spun into thread. Usually wool or synthetic fibers.

YOKE — That part of the garment designed to support pleats, gathers or bodice.

ZIG — The zig-zag stitch on the sewing machine.

ZIG OVERCASTING — Using the zig stitch to cover a raw edge.

Chapter 1

Preparing the Doll to Make a Basic Pattern

The method of marking a doll in order to measure and fit the clothes will vary with the doll.

Doll bodies come in a number of materials from wood to fine porcelain. Some porcelain dolls have cloth or leather bodies, and as you will be placing marks on the doll for measuring and fitting, the type of body will determine the type of marks.

We will discuss the cloth-bodied dolls first, beginning with the soft, cuddly baby doll, specifically the Bye-Lo, because most people will, at one time or another, dress a Bye-Lo doll. I do a few extra things to the basic commercial Bye-Lo body pattern that makes the body more desirable. The Bye-Lo pattern I'm talking about is the one with two-piece curved arms and frog-type legs.

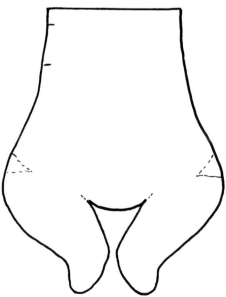

Frog type Bye-Lo baby body pattern with the two-piece curved arm.

If you are making an authentic antique reproduction doll, use unbleached muslin for the body. If you want to make the doll

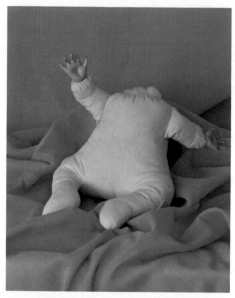

Bye-Lo baby body in unbleached muslin.

Bye-Lo body covered with flesh-colored tricot.

more appealing, use light pink or light flesh colored material.

I like to cut the body from muslin and soft pink or flesh colored tricot and then lay each piece of the muslin body on the wrong side of the corresponding piece of the tricot. After pinning them together, I machine stitch

around each piece close to the edge. I fold the front piece of the arm at the inside elbow area and sew in a dart, starting the dart about ⅛" from the edge and

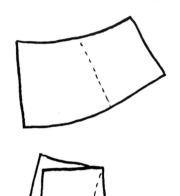

Fold the front section of the arm and sew a dart as indicated.

taper to ⅜" depth at the center, and back out to the outer edge. Sew the sleeves together down the sides only, making a tube. Slip the hand down the tube, wrist first, until you can see it at the wrist end. Before slipping the hand in place, however, you must decide whether you want the arms to extend upward or downward.

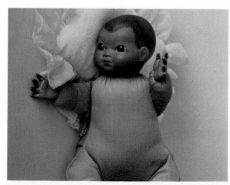

Tricot covered Bye-Lo body matching the doll's color, showing the arms in the up-reaching position.

I make mine reaching upward as that seems more natural. Check to make sure the hands are in correctly, remembering that when the arms are up, the palms will face the front and the thumbs will be to the head. The best way to get them right is to mark the front center of the arm tube at the wrist and then mark the front center of the doll's hand. Slip the hand through the tube, matching the marks and having the thumb toward the inside curve of the arm.

I hand sew a row of stitches ½" down from the wrist edge and, without cutting the double thread, I pull the stitching tight around the porcelain hand and then wrap the remaining thread around the area, over the stitching, several times. I secure the thread by stitching in one place several times and then I cut the thread. When threading your needle, be sure to allow enough thread for the above operation. A thin line of glue between the cloth and porcelain insures a secure joining.

The arm is now stuffed softly to within ¾" from the top and the edges are pinned together. They are placed on the front section of the body, edge on edge at the sewing line, again with the thumbs facing upward and the palms downward. I usually set the arms down 1" from the top of the body.

I then sew the body together. To make this easy, I pin the back and front crotch together at the center, I fit the feet together and pin them once through the center of the feet and once at the area of the back body - leg pleat or fold. I find it best to sew with the back part of the body on top. I clip the curved part of the seams, whether they curve in or out.

It helps the **in** curves so they will not pull or pucker, and helps the rounded or **out** curves to lay more smooth.

Doll with rounded joints; notice the flexibility.

After turning the body right side out, I stuff it softly through the leg and lower body area, with unbonded quilt batting. I use the unbonded batting because it is so soft and fluffy and never lumps, yet you can make the bodies firm. The upper part of the body should be stuffed firmly, but before I do that, there is one more thing I do to the body that is different. This can be done when you are cutting out the body.

I like my Bye-Lo baby's head to bend forward a little so I cut the front neck ½" lower at the center front and taper out to the side.

I hem the neck casing by hand, using double thread enclosing a cord; or use three or four strands of household string to make a cord. This is used to tie on the head and is inside the casing. I start at the center back and, after the casing is hemmed, I stuff the body quite firmly to enable the body to support the head. When completely stuffed, I place the neck of the head into the neck opening and tie the cord as tightly as possible. Shove the cord ends and knot down inside the body. Sometimes I have to use

the dull side of a table knife to get the knot inside.

When I am making a child doll with a cloth body, I don't often cover the muslin with tricot but use only the woven cloth. The arms and legs are joined together with stitching and glue, the same as the hands on the Bye-Lo. The elbows and knees are formed with a round joint that makes the doll more flexible than the traditional stitched across joint. To make a round joint, thread your needle so the thread is doubled and sew **around** the joint area after the arm or leg and cloth arm or leg tube are joined and stuffed to within ½"-¾" of the joint area. Pull the stitches tight and stitch through the same stitches again. This gives strength to the joint. If you want the joint more flexible, sew another row of stitches ¼" above the first row and pull it tight the same as

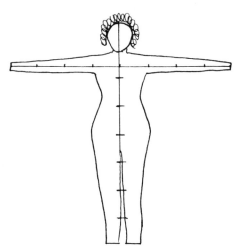

Diagram for proportioning a lady doll's figure. The control measurement is from the forehead to the bottom of the chin.

you did the first row. Finish by sewing in the same place several times and by clipping the thread end.

Complete your stuffing of the arm or leg and stitch it to the body. I suggest you leave an unstuffed section at the top of the leg so that the area is movable without being stiff.

Another cloth-bodied doll is the lady doll. If you have a lady doll head, hands and legs without a body pattern, don't dispair.

Make one using the method I use. First, determine your doll's height by the length of her face from her chin to her forehead. Times this measurement by eight. If her face measures 2" then the total doll should be 16", 2½" — 20", 3" — 24".

The doll pictured looks so lovely in a long dress that I went by the model's "ideal" measurement and made her 19" instead of 18. As a rule, models are tall and are considered "ideal" if their total height is not eight times but 8½ times their face length.

Measuring the shoulder-plate area to determine the body size for making a cloth body pattern.

Lady dolls usually have a shoulder plate, and to make a doll pattern, measure around the outside of the plate and add 1" for seams. This determines the width of the body at the top, allowing ¼" for each seam. I suggest you write that measurement on a piece of paper along with the following. Measure around the top of the leg and add ¾". This determines the size to make the leg pattern and allows the seams, plus ¼" for easing needed when attaching the cloth tube to the porcelain leg. Measure the arm the same way.

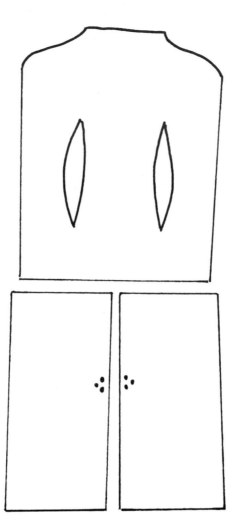

Cloth body and legs for a shoulder-plate lady doll.

The widest part of the hips should be twice the face measurement and the torso length is 3⅓ times the face length. The torso measurement is from the chin down, even though the shoulder plate extends down over the body. The arms are eight times the measurement of the face. Measure from fingertip across shoulderplate to the other fingertip.

To determine the length of the cloth part of the leg, add the face and the torso length. Subtract that figure from the total length. The resulting figure will be the length of the total leg. Subtract the porcelain part of the leg's length and you will have the measurement for the cloth tube length. Remember when making the pattern to allow the seams for joining to the leg and sewing to

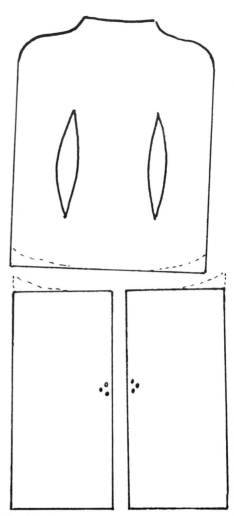

To give the bottom of the body a rounded look, cut the corners where indicated and add an equal amount to the leg at the side. the torso.

Generally the top of the cloth leg will measure ½ the width of the lower body so that when the legs are sewn to the torso, they will meet, not overlap at the center. Measure the arms the same way to determine the finished length but cut the tubes at least 1" longer so that you will have sufficient material to fold up over the shoulder.

Make darts at the waistline to control waist size. Usually the waist is 1¾ times the face size, down from the chin, but if you want her to be high-waisted, that's fine, put the waist high.

To give the doll a seat, cut a

Fish insert for a cloth body doll.

piece of cloth in the shape of a fish and sew it into the opening left at the bottom of the torso after the waist darts and side seams are sewn. For added shape, curve the center front and back of the bottom of the torso **down**, about ¼"-⅜", before sewing in the fish. This can be done by trimming off that amount from each side of the torso.

Remember, that if you cut ¼"-⅜" from the side of the doll's torso, you must add it to the side of the doll's leg. For two reasons: 1) the doll will be shorter, 2) the legs will spread apart at the feet too much. See illustration.

Firmly stuff the body, fold the top over like an envelope and stitch. Attach the arms and legs to the cloth tubes as described for the Bye-Lo hands; make a joint if one is needed. Close the leg tops and stitch to the torso at the front seam of the "fish." Stuff the arms, leaving an unstuffed area at the shoulder, so the arms will hang down, not stick out. Fold

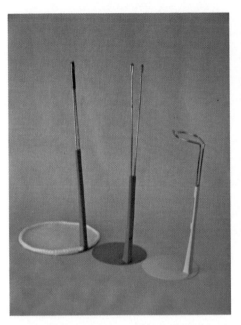

A doll stand with the curved part removed. The curved section can be straightened to make that part of the stand longer.

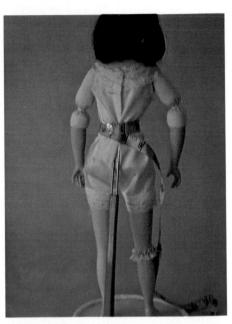

Always have the doll on a stand when measuring it for clothing if you want the stand to be unseen. Measure right over the stand and allow the extra in the cloths.

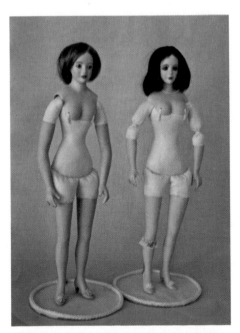

These two dolls are from the same mold — however one shoulder-plate spread more than the other in the bisque firing and therefore has a larger bust. This is why it is important to measure each shoulder-plate on the dolls so the bodies will fit.

Notice that one doll has more porcelain leg than the other.

the arm tube over lengthwise and stitch to torso top.

Sew a 2" piece of cloth tape through the holes in the shoulder plate and attach the head to the body. Sometimes I use selvage cut from the body material for the tape or, if I've covered the body with tricot, I use tricot or ribbon to attach the head portion of the doll.

When I put a doll on a doll stand, I don't want the stand to show unless it's necessary, and a shoulder plate on a doll is an excellent way to keep the doll upright and not have the stand show.

The commonly used stand has a base, a pole and a curved section that goes around the doll with a straight section that goes into the pole.

To make this stand practically invisible, I cut off the rounded or curved part of the stand where the curve meets the upright part. I discard the curved pieces and wrap masking tape over the cut ends to hold them together and make it easier to slip up the back of the doll, between the shoulder plate and body.

I then place the upright section of the stand in the stand pole and after adjusting it for proper height, I use a pair of pliers to pinch the pole so it will hold the upright part without letting it slip. I leave the doll on the stand when I measure her for clothes and include the stand in the measurements. That way the clothes (especially the slip and dress) cover the stand.

Sometimes shoulder plate doll bodies are made of leather and the leather extends up over the shoulder plate, making it impossible to use the stand that way — but the problem can be solved. I have put an upside-down pocket in the back of the leather body that holds the cut end of the upright section of the doll stand. And again, if that is not possible, a corset with a pocket will serve as well. Sometimes, depending upon the doll, these methods require some extra support. This support can be given by tying one or both legs to the stand pole with ribbon.

We are finally ready to mark our doll so we can measure her

for her clothes. Remember to have her on a stand if you want the stand concealed.

If your doll's body has a cleanable surface such as composition or porcelain, you can use a soft lead pencil for the marks and remove them afterwards with whatever works best. I find soap and water on a damp cloth, works very well for me.

determine what and where you will take the leg measurements.

The doll is now ready to have her clothing patterns drafted and her clothes made.

Marked dolls —
A doll marked with a soft lead pencil
A tape marked doll
A doll marked with yarn
Masking tape used to mark a doll

You can also use masking tape cut to a ⅛" for marking.

Narrow strips of cloth will work very well and serve as a base to which the garment can be pinned. A colored yarn is fine for marking cloth bodied dolls.

These are the marks you will need. Mark a line from the center front at the neckline down through the crotch and up the center back to the center back neckline. Mark another line down the side from the underarm to the ankle. Mark around the chest, waist, hips and at the leg joining and hips because sometimes this is the widest part of the body. Notice on the diagram that this measurement is horizontal to the crotch or body bottom. Mark across the crotch down the inseam on the leg. It's not necessary to mark around the arms and legs at this time because the length and style of the sleeve will determine the measurements of the arm, and what the garment will be can

Doll with an upside-down pocket on her leather body to accommodate the stand.

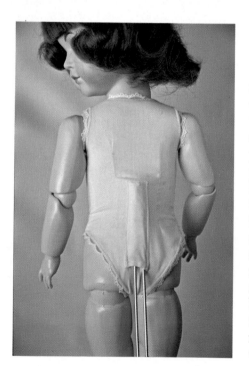

This doll has a body of Ultra Suede.

These dolls have the stand-up under the shoulder plate. Notice the spools to prevent broken legs.

Chapter 2

Pants, Pants and More Pants

Here we are with dolls without a stitch to their names, so let's take pity on them and make them some well-fitting clothes.

Why not start with pants? From one basic pattern we can make any style we want, from a bikini to long, ruffled pantaloons for girl dolls, and briefs to tailored tuxedo trousers for boy dolls.

Our doll is already marked, so measure the following places and draw equivalent lines on a piece of paper:

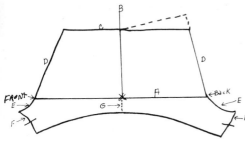

A basic pattern for pants using the body measurements. Seams need to be added.

A) The hip, from the center front around to the center back on the hip mark. Put an "F" at one of the line for front and a "B" at the other end for the back, and call this line A. Measure the hip from the center front to the side mark and mark an "X" on the line. Draw a perpendicular line at this X mark about ½ the length of the hip line (the length of this line is immaterial at this point).

Check the measurement from the side at the waist down to the hip and mark it on the line just drawn — remember, it's just to the hip line — call this line "B".

Now measure the waist from center front to center back, making a note of the side seams measurement from center front. Draw this line parallel to the hip line, making sure the side seam is at line B. This is line "C".

Measure up center front from hip mark to waist and connect waist and hip lines at the ends, call this line "D". Do the same up the center back from hip to waist. This line usually will be longer unless the doll has a fat tummy, so extend it up past the waist line and draw a line from the top end to the side seam on the waist line.

Now, measure at the center front down from the hip line to center of the crotch. Extend line D down past line A with an outward curved line the length of this measurement. Do the same with the back — again, this may be longer than the front. Call the lines "E".

Measure across the crotch and draw ½ the amount on an inward slant at the front and the back crotch lines. Call these lines "F".

After going this far, we need to decide what you will be making. If you are making underpants for a girl doll, decide how far you want them to be down the side. Measure and extend the side, mark B to the wanted length and make a mark "G".

Measure the inside leg where it joins the torso down to where you want the pants and add that length onto lines F. Now, draw a curved line from the end of the back F line meeting the mark on the side "BG", over to the end of the front F line.

This pattern will need ¼" seam allowance at the front and back and, as the measurement and lines are skin tight, you will need to also allow a little for ease depending on the material.

Because these pants fit snug, they will need an opening unless

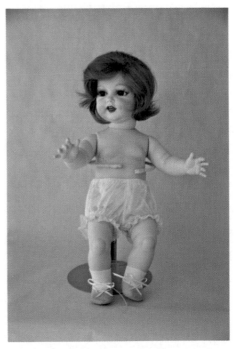

Semi-full panties with a leg ruffle and an elastic waist.

the waist is as large as the hips. You can see that if both front and back seams are sewn, you cannot get them on. To remedy this, we can add fullness and put elastic around the waist and legs. If making a placket, the waist can either have a waistband or be faced. If using a waistband, do not use a seam allowance on the waist as the waistband would be too high on the torso if you did. If using elastic, allow ½" for the elastic casing.

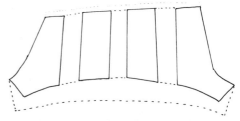

Enlarging the basic pattern for fullness including a short leg ruffle. A folded double cloth ruffle and casing can be made by adding double the ruffle and casing measurements.

On the smooth fitting panties, the leg can be finished either with a row of lace or can be hemmed. Allow for the hem. If you are zig-zaging the lace to the edge, if the lace is wider than ¼" (a seam) deduct the difference, otherwise the lace will hang down the leg farther than originally wanted.

To add fullness to the panties, widen the pants by cutting the pattern into four or five pieces and spacing them on a new paper to cut a pattern.

These pants do not have any leg fullness.

Allow for side seams and a casing, and decide if you want a ruffle on the leg. If you do, allow the width of the ruffle plus a hem on the ruffle; or, if you make a zig-overcast hem, you only need ⅛" to ³⁄₁₆" extra. I prefer lace on the ruffle so I add for the ruffle without subtracting for the lace because when the elastic is in the leg I like the pants to blouse a little.

Because the garments are small, I prefer not to have the extra bulk of a casing for the leg elastic so I encase the elastic with a wide zig stitch. Method: Use ⅛" elastic, and from a length of elastic measure and mark the stretched size of elastic needed

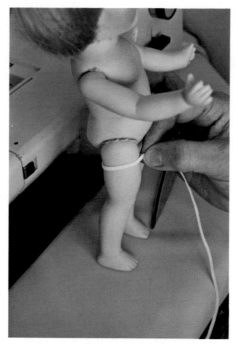

Measuring elastic around the doll's leg, notice that the elastic is stretched.

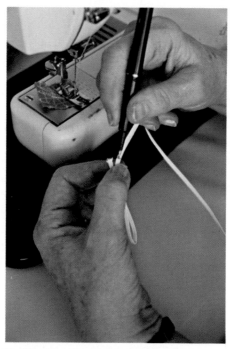

Marking the elastic for correct size.

but **do not** cut the elastic in the proper lengths at this time. Leave them connected to the bolt or length of elastic.

Now either hem, overcast or sew lace to the leg bottom. Place the pants, right side down, under the pressure foot with the needle at the elastic line.

Set the straight stitch length on the shortest stitch and sew

the elastic to the pants on the elastic line for about ⅜", ending with the needle down into the elastic and fabric.

Placing the pants leg under the pressure foot with the right side down. Notice how the machine stitching will start from a scrap of material already under the foot.

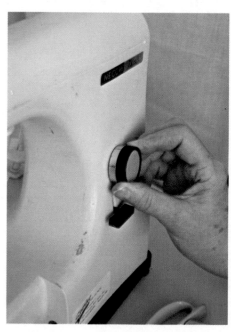

Adjusting the machine to a zig stitch.

Now set the zig stitch on the widest setting, leaving the stitch length on the shortest stitch, and sew over the elastic on the elastic line, covering the elastic but not catching any elastic. If you pull the elastic as you sew, it will work very well. When you are within ³⁄₁₆″ of the end of the pants, release the pressure foot and make sure the measured mark on the elastic is right on the edge. Turn the zig stitch back to straight, leave the stitch length short and sew the balance of the elastic to the first pant leg.

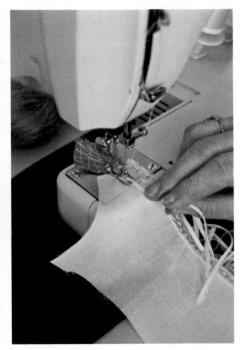

Stitching the elastic to the pants.

Enclosing the elastic in a zig casing.
Continuing to the other leg without cutting the elastic.

Place the other leg under the pressure foot with the edge to

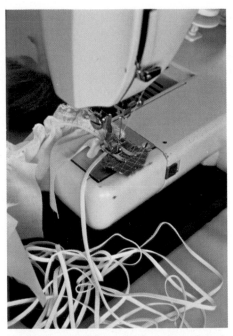

Ending the stitching onto the scrap of cloth.

With the elastic cut.

the mark on the elastic and stitch for ¼″ or ⅜″, then change to the widest zig stitch and finish as the first leg. This method is very good on baby-doll dress sleeves. I usually use ¼″ elastic at the waist in a hem.

In making long pants you can have a side seam. And usually, long pants will be on a doll with a slim waist. To make them fit well, darts will be needed, so

when drawing a pattern, draw the waist the same size as the hips and deduct the darts to get the waist size. (See illustration.)

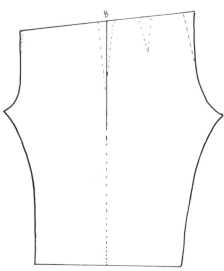

Long trousers with darts to make a fitted waist.

To make the pattern, proceed as far as for the panties, with the exception of the above mentioned waist measurement. Draw the side measurement down to the ankle or whatever length is wanted. Decide on the width at the bottom of the pants and draw a line of that measurement at the bottom of line B, parallel to line A, with ½″ on the front side of line B and the other ½″ to the back. Extend the D or inseam lines down to meet the ends of the bottom line.

When making male doll trousers you can make the pattern two ways. One way is to cut out the pattern, with seam allowances, from paper towels. Pin the pattern on the doll, pinning one waist dart in the back, one waist dart on the side seam and, if needed, a small pleat or dart in the front part. Make any corrections in the leg width. Some of this correction, if needed, can be made on the outside seam. Remove the pant leg from the doll, cut away the dart and correction area, and split down the side. Make the pattern,

—15—

allowing seams where needed. Side pockets and a turn back for the fly can also be added.

These trousers look nice with a front opening. However, at times the material may be too heavy and a front opening is very bulky. When this happens, I usually make the pants look like they close in the front but I actually close them in the back.

Another way to make the pants is to split the pants down the side seam, cutting a V-shaped section off the front side seam (equivalent to a dart). Make the side pockets or simulate them with stitches and sew the side seams together. Make a simulated fly by folding the front back and top stitching. Sew the back seam and cut a waistband the size of the pant's waist — not the doll's waist. Sew the waistband on, enclosing enough elastic to fit the doll's waist. These pants can slip on the doll without an opening. Sometimes they look better if the elastic is across the back only.

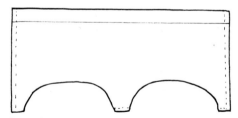
One piece panties with elastic in the waist.

Another simple panty is made in one piece and doesn't have any fullness, but does have elastic at the waist and the panties slip on. Notice the diagram and make them the size to fit your doll.

To Make a Romper Suit

A leotard can be made with two seams, one at the back and the other for legs and crotch. They are cut the same as the panties just described except the front crotch is made very narrow and the back crotch is tucked to fit the bottom. The legs are

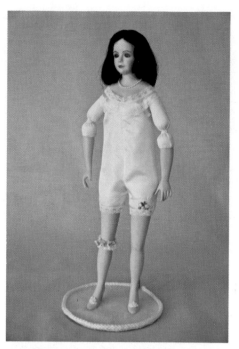
The "Teddy" style of underwear.

Underpants worn in a bygone era called pantaloons; some had an open crotch.

cut long enough to fit over the feet.

Some old-fashioned dolls have pantaloons with a split crotch — apparently ladies wore them like that because doll fashions were copied from the clothing of the period in which they were dressed. It's very interesting to note some of the construction of these old garments. Many under-garments

were closed with buttons. Often the pants had a waistband that buttoned on each side or was attached to a panty; waist in the front and had a drop seat at the back that buttoned onto the back of the panty waist.

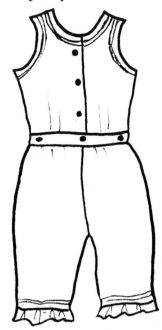
Panty-waist with drop seat pant attached.

When making the doll's pants, determine the style by the dress it will wear. The square dancer's pants are very full and help hold out her slips and dress. The baby dolls with bent legs need fullness

One piece underpants.

— not only to look pretty but to fit nicely over their seat.

This modern-day lady has such lovely legs it's a shame to use only panties for her cloth bottom so I put her in a "Teddy" suit of underwear that covers most of her cloth body.

To make a romper suit, combine the information for making pants with the instructions for dresses or blouses.

There are many styles of boy doll's pants, some are knee pants, some short, some full.

A pair of bloomers.

More are mentioned in Chapter 7.

After making the first drawn draft of a pattern, cut it in paper towelling with the added seams and fit it to the doll.

If adjustments are needed, do them, and draw the final pattern on sturdy paper. After using the pattern, it's wise to place it in an envelope with a sample of the material used and any comments on the use of that pattern, including the size doll the pattern fits.

Chapter 3

Underthings — Slips, Corsets and Petticoats

To make a pattern for a slip, which is an undergarment that has a bodice as well as a skirt, with the bodice and skirt cut in one piece we will use the upper torso marks.

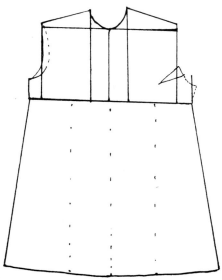

Diagram for the slip using the body measurements and showing the armhole dart.

Often on dolls, the front and back of the slip are made the same regardless of fit. We will find in custom dressing the doll, however, that there can be a big difference between the front and back. Therefore, let's make the front pattern first. Measure the chest, across the front, from one underarm mark to the other, and draw a line that length on a piece of paper. Put a mark at the center of the line and measure up from that center mark to the neck. Measure out toward the arm from that line, at the neck, and draw a line parallel to the chest line from the arm joining to the other arm joining.

Measure straight **up** from the chest line to the shoulder line at the neck and draw this line on the paper. Now measure **up** from the chest line to the shoulder line at the arm joining. Draw this line

A slip with a yoke.

in the proper place on the paper, keeping it an even distance from the first chest-to-shoulder drawn line. Join the top of the two shoulder lines from arm to neck.

Measure the underarm side seam down from the arm joining to the chest line and draw this line up from each end of the chest line. Draw a curve from this line up to the shoulder line. This line may need to be curved more, but can be corrected when fitting the pattern.

Also, you may find that a dart will be needed in the front armhole so that the slip will fit well and not have a tendency to poke out at the bottom of the skirt. Yes, an armhole dart can correct that problem.

Finish the front pattern by drawing the length needed, measuring from the chest mark down. Allow more width at the bottom by drawing the side on an A-line slant.

Now cut out the pattern and fit it to the front of the doll. Often, because of the doll's shape, the pattern will poke out at the bot-

Simple "A" line slip with ruffle added.

A slip on a yoke.

tom; correct this with a dart about ⅔ of the way down from the shoulder, in the armseye. By making the dart, you will shorten the armseye, so simply cut the curve lower at the side seam to make the armseye long enough.

This dart will make very little, if any, difference in the length of the skirt.

Make the back pattern the same way and have it open down the back for ease in putting it on the doll. An arm dart will not be needed in the back.

The slip back can be open all the way or only part of the way —depending on the doll.

To sew the slip I first determine the dress neck so the finished slip neck will not show. After cutting the neck's shape to match the dress, I sew the shoulder seams. Most often I finish the neck and armholes with lace that I sew on with a short zig-zag stitch, keeping the stitches fairly close together. Experiment on a scrap of material to get the proper setting.

Just a word here about what I do to the lace before zigging it to the slip. If you look at a piece of regular lace you will see a scalloped or fancy edge (unless it is insertion), and a straight edge. This straight edge will, if it is cotton, have a heavier thread to pull for gathering. This fine lace deserves to be handstitched to the garment. But if your lace is like the majority of the lace to-day, it will not have a gathering thread, rather it will have two rows of a straight thread with what looks like tiny ladder rungs between the two threads.

When this edge is zigged to the slip, I find it isn't as pretty as I want it to be, so I carefully cut off the first row of thread through the rung area and then zig the lace to the slip, covering the second thread line. So the lace will not show beyond the neck line, I set the lace down on the material so the edge of the material show at the fancy edge of the lace. Then after stitching, the excess slip material can be cut away and the zig stitch will prevent it from fraying. After sewing the side seams, a slightly gathered lace can be zigged around the bottom.

If I'm gathering the lace, I do not cut off the first heavy thread, but I do machine stitch a row of gathering between the two threads and make the zig stitch a little wider to cover both threads on the lace.

Placement of lace to keep the armseye the original size.

Cutting the excess material from behind the lace after it has been stitched to the garment edge.

the slip and the lace on the ruffle are even. Cover the raw edge of the ruffle with a row of lace or ribbon.

One method of stitching a ruffle to a slip.

Slip with back ruffle only.

Sometimes the ruffle can be sewn on with the right side of the ruffle to the right side of the slip and the lace edge up toward the shoulders. After stitching the ruffle to the slip at the gathering line, fold the ruffle down and gently press the ruffle at the stitching line so it will hang down nicely and be even with the bottom of the slip.

On some dresses the front will hang straight and have fullness at

Simple "A" line slip with a bottom ruffle.

You may want a ruffle on the slip to add prettiness, so subtract for the ruffle on the pattern, but remember the seams. If you want the ruffle to help hold out the dress skirt, make the slip the length needed and finish the bottom with lace. Then, make a separate lace-edged ruffle and sew it onto the slip so that the lace on

the back. For this style make a slip with gathered fullness at the back only.

Slip with a low back ruffle.

Slip skirt gathered to a bodice at the natural waistline.

A crinoline-type layered petticoat.

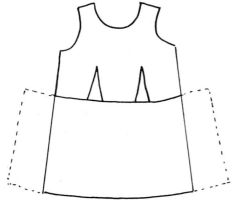

Diagram for cutting a slip with a natural waistline with darts in the bodice. Remember to add the seams.

A short bouffant slip of many layers of full gathered net. Notice how the ruffles are near the same length at the bottom.

A petticoat of eyelet trimmed with ribbon, showing the chemise.

gathered rows with all of the bottoms of the rows even, one with another.

Sometimes a slip will have a gathered skirt and a fitted waist. Simply make the top of the slip pattern the same way as instructed but cut it off at the waist, dart in the excess material with two darts at the front and two in the back. Sometimes, if the tummy is chubby, only back darts are needed. Add a gathered skirt to complete this type of slip. The skirt will hold out the dress very well if it's the same width as the dress skirt. If a less bouffant look is wanted, make the slip skirt less full.

The petticoat does not have a bodice, and hangs from the waist with a waistband and can be short, long, slim, full or multi-layered.

Our square dancer wears a petticoat with layers of gathered fine net to form a crinoline. These are also worn under full skirts that need to have the fullness emphasized. The net is cut different widths and sewn on in

On one such skirt, I also stitched several thicknesses of horsehair braid in rows to act as hoops.

When petticoats are worn, it's nice to also make a chemise for the doll. This is a bodice covering that can be like a slip that ex-

This slip has a ruffle sewn on the top of the skirt for extra fullness.

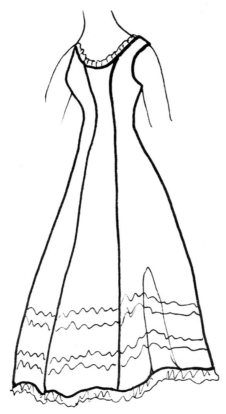

A princess line slip.

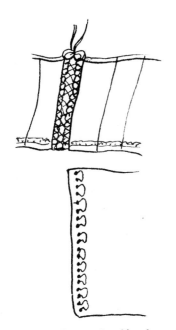

Using the eyes from sets of hooks and eyes for lacing a doll's corset.

corset.

Hand sew the other layer ends to the first layer, enclosing the stitching on the loops so when the layers are turned right side out, only the loop will show. Do not sew the top or bottom of the corset together until it has been turned. After turning, bind the top and bottom with self material, lace or ribbon. Trim as desired with rows of stitching to give the appearance of a reinforced corset. Lace in the back or front through the loops with ribbon. Oh yes! Did you think to deduct from the overall size of the corset to allow for the lacing and loops? I'm sorry I didn't mention it before, but part of the purpose of this book is to help you think things out for yourself in regards to clothing construction.

tends past the waist. It can be made with straps if so desired.

Dolls really don't need corsets, but to authentically dress a doll in clothing of the period when they wore corsets, one must subject the doll to a corset. These can be made by fitting a straight piece of material around the doll at the corset area and pinning darts where needed. Cut two layers and sew the darts in, each separately. Hand sew a row of the loop part of hook and eyes to each side of one layer of the corset. Place them on the end, close together, with the loop facing in. These are the lacing holes for the

Remember, period underclothing is held together with buttons or drawstrings.

For a fitted slip, make darts at the waistline, or cut it in a princess style. See Chapter 4 for instructions on princess cut.

Making Doll Dresses

There are so many different dresses that it's difficult to know where to start. Perhaps if we make a basic pattern, we can branch out and create a short-waisted dress, a long-waisted dress, a natural-waisted dress, a princess-style dress and a beautiful bridal gown.

This gored dress has lace for the bodice as well as for the skirt trim.

A simple dress with a touch of lace.

Always remember that these pattern drafts are exact to the doll's measurements and a trial pattern should be cut from paper towels, with the seams added. This paper pattern should be tried on the doll over her under-things and any adjustments made before making the final pattern. One adjustment could be to allow a little extra for a looser fit.

Again, our doll is shaped differently in the front than in the back, so let's do the front first. Measure the front chest and draw a line that length on a piece of paper; mark the center. Measure the front chest and draw a line that length on a piece of paper; mark the center. Measure from the chest measurement

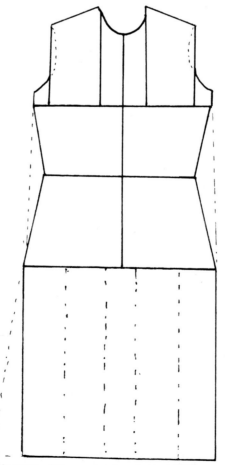

Diagram for a basic dress with an allowance for a full waist that can be belted. Remember the seam allowances.

down to the hip line and draw a line straight down from the center of the chest line. Now measure the front hip line and draw it parallel to the chest line.

Do the same with the waist, centering it on the center line and spacing it in the right place between the hip and chest line. Draw a line from the ends of chest line down to the waist and down to the ends of the hip line. Extend the center line up, as far as the neck, the proper length. Do the same along the arm joining to the shoulder. This is the same procedure used to make the slip pattern. Measure from the underarm to the chest line and extend that amount up from the chest line. Make a curved line for the armseye. Join the neck marks with a curved line for the neck. Measure the skirt length and complete the skirt by measuring down in several places along the hip line.

If you want a simple sheath dress with a belted waist, straighten the line at the waist by drawing a straight line at the side from the chest line to the hip line.

Sometimes, the doll's front will require a dart to fit better over the bust. If so, pin one in under the arm, either straight across or slanting up from just

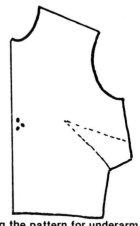

Adjusting the pattern for underarm darts.

Underarm darts.

above the waistline. If you pin it in on a slant, you will notice that the side seam will not be even, so add a piece of paper to the pattern and fill out the pattern. Also the dart will take up side length, so adjust that. After the front is finished, make the back pattern the same way except for the dart. Make the side seams the same length on the back as the front.

The back can be split down the center for an opening, either all the way and a lap over for the closing, or only part way and a separate placket sewn into the opening. If the dress is to open down the front, then split the front wherever you plan to have the opening.

Decide on the sleeve length and style and make a rough draft by measuring around the arm at the length wanted, and draw a line across on a piece of paper. Mark the right end **front** and the left end **back**. Let's make a short sleeve to begin with.

Measure the length of the sleeve from the shoulder to the wanted length and draw a line up from the center of the first line which is the arm measurement at the wanted sleeve length. Measure around the armseye and allow ½″ for easing. (This is for a doll 14″-18″ in height.) Allow more for a larger doll and less for a smaller. Keep this measurement in mind while measuring the underarm at the length line up to the joining of the underarm

to the body. Make a line up from each end of the width of the arm line and draw a straight line across, joining the two lines from left to right parallel to the first line drawn.

Now, take ½ of the armseye measurement and, starting at the top of the center line, draw a rounded outward curve half-way down to the underarm line at the back, and an inward curve the rest of the way. Draw the same line on the front side, making the inward curve a little deeper. If you meet the underarm line before you run out of armseye measurement, don't stop, continue until the measurement is reached and connect the end of the armseye line to the bottom of the sleeve line. If you run out of the armseye measurement before you reach the underarm line, continue until the two lines meet. This is a simple plain sleeve with no puff, only a nice roll over the shoulder area. The roll is achieved by sewing a gathering thread on the seam line and ease in the fullness over the shoulder.

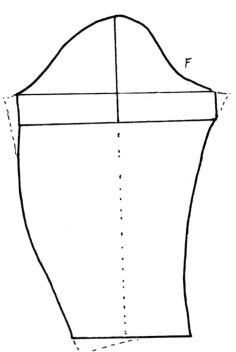

Diagram for making a pattern for a long or short fitted sleeve.

If a long sleeve is wanted and the elbow is slightly bent or the

doll is jointed and can bend her elbow, make the sleeve the same way. In addition, draw the wrist width line more to the front so that when connecting the side sleeve lines the back line will slant to the wrist making a curve in the back side of the sleeve. This makes the back side longer so you can ease in the extra material at the elbow area.

A full puffed sleeve from the basic pattern.

To make a puffed sleeve with all the puff in the armhole part of the sleeve, split the sleeve from the top to the elbow area and spread it like a fan. When cutting the pattern, allow extra length at the top of the sleeve so the fullness will be both up and around.

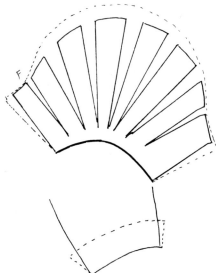

Drafting the sleeve like this will give you all the fullness in the armseye, mainly through the top area, and can be gathered or pleated.

To make a short puffed sleeve with most of the fullness in the bottom part of the sleeve, cut the sleeve pattern fan-like from the bottom. For fullness at both top and bottom, cut the pattern into several pieces and spread them

—23—

for a new pattern, allowing extra length through the center area only. Do not add extra length under the arm. If you are having a self ruffle on the sleeve, the fullness added to the sleeve can form the ruffle, so allow the extra length.

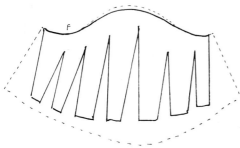

This sleeve has fullness at the bottom only. A long sleeve with fullness at the wrist can be drafted the same way.

Another style of dress is the natural-waisted type. Make the basic pattern the same way, including the enlarged waistline. Cut the pattern at the waist and make darts in the front and back to make the waist fit. If the skirt is full and/or the material bulky, it is necessary to allow an extra amount in the waist size to accommodate this bulkiness. To avoid more bulkiness at the waist, lower the slip waist so the gathered slip waist and the

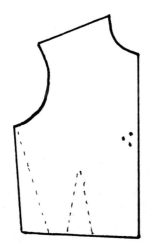

Pattern diagram allowing for waist darts.

gathered dress waist will not be on top of each other.

A high-waisted dress can have the bodice down to just under the arm. A dress of this type — one with a yoke, is explained in

Chapter 10.

A doll with a figure, or a lady doll, looks very nice in a princess style dress because her shape can be revealed without darts, and the princess lines are beautiful.

When making a princess pattern, I use the drape method in combination with the line drawing method. First draft the pattern in the regular way with line drawings, making it as long as the dress is to be. Split the pattern on each side all the way down from the center of the shoulder to the bottom, and lay the pattern on a piece of muslin or old sheeting with an allowance of 1″ between the cut pieces. Fold the material in the center lengthwise and cut it on the fold of the material, then both sides will be the same.

Pin the material with the front crease to the center front of the doll and the back crease to the center back of the doll. Pin the sides together at each underarm,

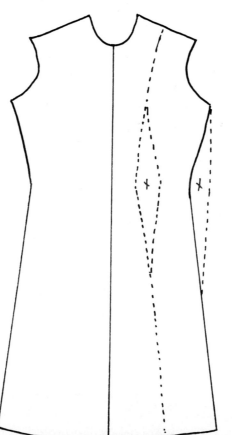

Cutting princess lines on the basic pattern.

with a ¼″ seam.

Now, pinch the material between the center front and the side seam at the waistline, together, and pin it about an equal distance from the center and the side. Pin the shoulder seams together at each end. Continue pinning the pinch seam up over the bust to the shoulder, allowing the dress to lay flat and smooth over the bust to the waist without any puckers.

Pin from the waist down to form a dart. Any more fullness that will be needed can be put in when making the final pattern. Pin the back the same way, matching the pinch lines at the shoulder. If you wish, you can pin only one side and make a pattern to be cut on the fold for the center panel. To make the half pattern, unpin the cloth pattern at the center front and back creases and cut them along the crease.

Discard the one side and re-

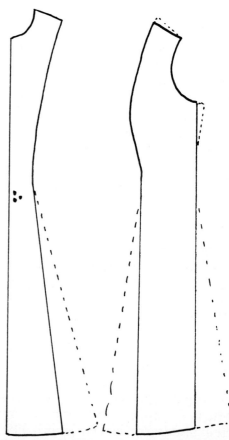

Note the addition to the skirt for fullness.

—24—

move the pinned side. Cut off the excess pinched material, leaving a seam allowance. Also pin and trim any excess from the side waistline if it was necessary to take part of the waist in at the side seams.

On the pinch seam, make two notches, one at the waist and one between the shoulder and waist so when you are sewing the dress these notches can be matched and the dress fit as it was pinned.

Unpin the half pattern and split the skirt from the end of the dart to the bottom. Lay the center piece of the cloth pattern on the edge of the pattern paper and draw around the pattern until you get to the end of the dart. Place a ruler along the angle of the dart and increase the fullness of the skirt from the end of the dart to the bottom of the dress.

Place the cloth side panel on a piece of paper and draw around the pattern until you get to the dart. Increase that side the same as the front panel. If the side seam needs more fullness, increase the same way.

The pincesss style is lovely in slips, dresses, formals, wedding gowns and coats. The draped effect on some of the antique patterns is an extension of a princess panel.

How to sew ruffles on a skirt is described in Chapter 8, but the skirt underneath isn't mentioned.

It's best to use a gored skirt for underneath ruffles. The princess skirt is a gored skirt and should be made less full around the bottom when using ruffles.

Or an entirely different method can be used for making a skirt that will hide all the raw edges. That skirt is made in tiers. Starting at the top, sew a ruffle to a piece of material 1½ times the waist measurement and 1″ shorter than the finished ruffle. (This 1″ measurement is for a doll 16″ and taller, a smaller doll would use less.)

The second ruffle is sewn to a piece of material two times longer than the waist and 1″ shorter than the finished ruffle. The third ruffle is sewn to a piece three times larger than the waist and the **same** length as the finished ruffle. This is the bottom ruffle. Now, gather and sew the bottom ruffle and under-ruffle to the bottom of the second under-ruffle piece. Then gather the second ruffle and under-ruffle and sew them to the top under-ruffle.

The top ruffle and under-ruffle are then gathered and sewn to the waist. The back seam can then be sewn together sewing the ruffles separately most of the way and leaving an opening for dressing the doll. When the ruffles are sewn to the under-ruffle piece, use a long stitch that can be pulled to gather the ruffle and under-ruffle for sewing to the next part.

Look at pictures of dresses and study them for construction. A princess dress with gathers over the bust on the side panel only can be made by cutting that part of the pattern in a fan shape and gathering the fanned edge in the fabric. Then sew in place, matching the notches. A dress with an overskirt that tapers up to the waist can be cut from the skirt pattern to the desired tapering line.

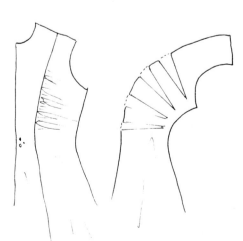

Adding gathered fullness over the bust for style.

A princess dress can have several panels using the method given.

Pinafores can be made from the same pattern as the dress. The ruffle gives it a fuller look.

This dress with a shirred front was made using the princess cut. Another way to get the same effect is to place the shirred section over a basic bodice and cover the edges with trim.

A pinafore can be made from a dress pattern by lowering the neckline.

When making a dress with a shirred bodice, use the following method. Using lining material or a piece of the dress material, cut from the basic pattern a bodice the size required — be it a yoke or a longer bodice. Set it to one side. It is the control piece. Now cut the yoke or bodice pattern in several strips and make a new pattern by separating the strips until they measure at least twice the width of the bodice — 2½-3 times makes a lovely fullness. Add the skirt length and cut the pattern allowing the seams and hem.

Fold the pattern in half through the center and place it on the fold of the material, making sure the material is even. With a contrasting thread, hand sew a line through the bodice from center neck to the center at the last row of shirring. This will enable you to center the shirred bodice to the center of the control piece and not have the bodice offside. The colored thread can be removed later.

Mark the first or bottom row of shirring with pins or chalk, or another way is to press in a creased row. Set the length of the stitch longer than regular sewing and sew along the marked row. Determine the distance you want between the rows and sew the additional rows that distance apart. Pull the back threads, arranging the shirring evenly. Pull two or three rows at a time until the shirring fits the control. Do the back bodice pieces the same, stitch together around the edge of the control, arranging the gathers evenly. There may be excess dress material at the neckline that can be cut off after the control and shirring are stitched.

Hand catch the bottom of the control piece to the bottom row of shirring. Complete stitching the dress together and trim as desired. A binding around the neck looks nice, and a bit of gathered lace will make it look even nicer.

French dresses: These styles are varied and sometimes appear to be complicated, so for your first French style, make it simple but with a French flair.

To plan bodice length, divide the total garment length into three equal parts and use two parts for the bodice and one part for the skirt length. Often the French styles have pleated skirts, so to determine the amount of material needed, measure around the bottom of the finished bodice. Add to that twice the amount of material needed, measure around the bottom of the finished bodice. Add to that twice the amount of material. For example: The bottom of the bodice measurement is 12" so add 24", a total of 36".

You can make 24½" pleats. This will take all the material, so add for seams. I usually add a couple of inches for good measure. Sometimes it will need to be twice the length plus waist seam allowance. Nothing is needed for a hem. Press the material double lengthwise and machine stitch the two raw edges together.

It's nice if you have a pleater, but if not don't worry. You can pleat using the following method. Measure and mark the top of the skirt for ½" pleats by starting at the right end if you want the pleats folded to the right, and the left if you want the pleats folded to the left. Place the first mark, using a pencil or tailoring chalk, 1" from the edge.

The next mark is ½", then 1", all across the skirt top until you have the required number. Now make corresponding marks using pins along the bottom of the skirt. Fold the chalk marks at the top over to form the pleats and machine stitch them in place.

Place the pleated skirt on the ironing board, and pin the stitched edge to the board, now fold and pin the bottom pleats to

match the top pleats, and pin them to the board. Press the pleats with the iron and remove the bottom pins. Press again to remove any pin holes.

Your pressing will depend upon the type of material, so determine the iron setting by using a scrap of material. You may need a pressing cloth, either damp or dry, a steam or dry iron, or you may find that pressing on the wrong side is best. It isn't necessary to always have the skirt double, and sometimes two skirts look very nice; one can be either pleated or gathered lace.

You can make the dress look like it has a jacket by using a different material for part of the bodice or covering the bodice with lace.

A gathered or shirred panel down the front of the bodice seems to be a must on this type of French fashion. A sash and cuffs will add trim.

To make a cuff that gives the look of being a little larger than the sleeve, trace around the bottom part of the sleeve, both across the bottom and up each side to the width you desire the cuff to be. Remove the sleeve and

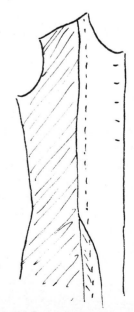

Press the facing and lining seam to one side rather than open.

draw across the paper with a slight curved line on the top of the cuff, now extend the top line at each end about ¼" and draw a line from this new top line end down to the bottom of the cuff. Cut two for each sleeve and seam each piece into a ring. Sew two of the rings together at the top for each sleeve. Clip in several places and turn.

Press and sew to finished sleeve by putting the right side of the cuff to the wrong side of the sleeve, matching the seams and stitching together. Clip again in two or three places and turn the cuff to the outside.

I find that this seam will lay better and look more tailored if I lay it to one side and top stitch close to the seam on the sleeve part of the dress. If the dress material is soft, line it with taffeta, crinoline or even muslin to give it body. The two can be sewn as one for a neater look.

Many French styles had beautiful treatment at the back with draping and bows.

I find that if I make the back bodice and then either fold bias material into a drape and add it to the back or extend the front

Becky in a child's German-style outfit.

part of the bodice into a drape and bring it around to the center back, that the effect is beautiful.

I suggest that you try it first in muslin to get the effect you want.

German doll dresses — The Germans were the first to make character dolls, and some of the most beloved and sought after antique dolls are these pre-World War I German character dolls. The lovely Hilda is one such doll. She is presented as a baby, a toddler and a child, with appropriate clothing to her age.

Pouties were often presented in peasant-type dresses, and our Becky is a wholesome example of a child doll. She has a porcelain head and arms with a cloth body and legs. She wears drawers, a slip of cotton and a dress fashioned from a remnant from a drapery shop. The slip, dress and pinafore are high-waisted, and I used the same basic pattern for all three.

Her long sleeves are gathered into a band and, as her hands are quite slender, I was able to slip her sleeves on without having an opening, with the snaps in the wrist band. However, if a placket

is needed, allow enough extra material in the cuff to lap over and close with buttons or snaps.

The bodice is trimmed with tucks every ½", so extra material should be allowed for tucks. For tucked sleeves or bodice, tuck and press the material first before cutting.

The neck band has an inner-facing which was placed between the front piece and the lining and

BeBe Jumeau and friend.

This bride is in ivory, combining material and lace.

enough that you dress your doll to fit its category. A chubby child or toddler doll dressed as a bride can only remind one of a child playing grown up, whereas nothing looks lovelier than a lady doll dressed as a lady in a gorgeous formal or a beautiful bridal gown.

A train will enhance a bridal gown and should be allowed for, not only in the dress and lining but in the slip as well, providing the dress is bouffant.

Remember to fit the dress skirt over underthings so you can cut the skirt full enough to hang well over the slip. To determine how far back you want the train to trail, place the doll on her stand, and either hold the material which is to hang down from the waist, or measure from the waist with a measuring tape for the length. When making a bridal veil, make sure it adds to and enhances the total picture.

When making a pattern that is the same for the right side of the doll as the left side, make half of the pattern only and cut it on the fold as needed. The total pattern can be used for fitting if desired but a half pattern is sufficient.

sewn with the front piece for re-inforcement.

Her pinafore material has rows of embroidered flowers or motifs that offer a guideline for the tucks. Notice the different tuck sizes.

Although the pinafore skirt is the same width as the dress, the addition of a ruffle gives the effect of more fullness. This pina-

This veil complements the gown.

Notice how this lovely tucked bodice looks like a yoke due to the placing of the ruffle. Also notice the three-tiered skirt.

fore has an all-around skirt that is seamed in the back. Embroidered eyelet forms the pinafore bodice and was placed on the pattern and the corners mitered and stitched before the entire bodice was cut out. A rosebud and a bit of ribbon matching the dress trim complete the pinafore.

Brides — I cannot emphasize

Ruffles.

Handmade clothing.

A shirred skirt. Doll by Loree Wolfe.

Using a color under a sheer fabric.

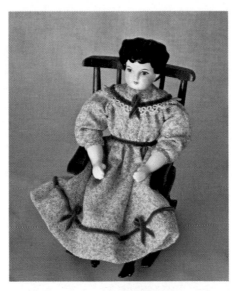

A simple dress for a China doll.

"Little Mary" made and dressed by Karen Hansen.

A special shaped sleeve for a curved arm doll. Refer to line drawing.

The yoke look is achieved with a ruffle.

Another ruffle yoke with the ruffle re-enforced with plain material, the sleeves are made with two layers of material for body.

A bevy of brides.

This sleeve is lined tulle to give it a bouffant look.

The ruffle on this sleeve is cut on the bias and gathered through the center and stitched to the sleeve on the gathering line to form a double ruffle.

Notice the lace at the neckline. Motifs from this same lace have been cut and appliqued to the skirt and veil.

The under skirt has two rows of ribbon that enhance the dress by showing through the top skirt.

The lace is trimmed with pearls.

Another bride from the same mold.

Chapter 5

Outerwear — Coats and Jackets

Baby Coats

A coat with a bonnet to match can make a charming baby outfit, and a matching dress underneath makes it doubly attractive. To make the one pictured, use a very nice piece of material. I used a fairly heavy piece of silk that I had saved for 25 years. Even though it was heavy in comparison to the fine shantung-weave silk of the gown, it still needed an inner facing for body.

This complete outfit is made of silk. The coat is lined and inner lined.

The pattern was fitted over the dress and then three pieces of each pattern were cut, one in the lovely coat material, one in an inner lining, and one in the lining material. The coat and inner lining were sewn as one.

To make a coat like this for your doll, make a basic pattern with a front opening. It has an overlap in the bodice only, so allow for that. The bodice is not a yoke. It extends down under the sleeve about 1½". The collar is made by pinning the bodice pattern pieces together at the shoulder. (Again I mention using only half the pattern. Heretofore, we have had the closing in the back, but this is to be a front closure so remember that when doing the pattern.)

Back to the collar. After the shoulders are pinned together, place the bodice center back on the straight edge of a piece of paper and pin it even with the edge. Lay the rest of the bodice flat and trace around the neck to the center front. Remove the pins and take the bodice from the paper and mark out from the neck the size you want the collar to be.

Draw a curved line for a curved collar front, and a squared corner for that type of collar front. This collar will lay flat. If you want the collar to roll and stand up a little, slit the collar from the outside in toward the neck, about at the half way point around the collar half, and lap the outside edge of the collar over at the slit. A ¼" overlap should be enough, if not, lap it more.

The cape is cut from paper made in a doughnut shape, darts are taken at the shoulder and the front is curved to look nice. The neck of the darted cape fits the neck of the coat and collar. The sleeves are long and have cuffs, and the cape, cuffs and all around the skirt are trimmed with a peak made of the coat material. This trim is explained in Chapter 8 and is sewn to the skirt after the side seams have been sewn together. The lining is also sewn to the skirt part of the coat at this time. The seams are clipped and the excess material at each corner cut off and the skirt turned right side out and pressed.

The raw edges at the waistline are matched and two gathering stitches sewn across the top, about ¼" apart. Finish the cape in like manner, and finish the collar the same except there isn't any pointed trim on the collar. Be sure you sewed the coat and inner lining as one.

After the shoulder seams are sewn together, both in the coat and the lining, sew the lining to the coat facing. I hope you have pressed everything along the way.

The side seams and shoulder seams are best when pressed open (and the lining and facing seam pressed to the lining side). Place the neck of the cape with the right side out on the right wide of the bodice neck line, and pin in place. Now, put the collar right side up over the cape and pin it also.

Place the lining-facing section over the collar section and stitch them all together, being careful to not get any little tucks and unwanted pleats in the neckline because there are quite a number of thicknesses. Clip to the stitching in several places so when the bodice is turned right side out, it will lay flat. To help it lay flat and to also add a bit of decoration, I usually hand sew a row of continuous cross stitches close to the seam. This isn't really necessary, but it does look nice and will give you a feeling of satisfaction to know how nice the inside of the garment looks.

Make the cuff and place it on the bottom of the sleeve tube with the lining side to the right side of the sleeve.

Pin the bottom part of the sleeve lining tube over the cuff and stitch all three together along the raw edges.

Clip the seam in several places and turn the lining up inside the sleeve. Again a decorative stitch looks nice on the lining close to the seam.

Sew the underarm side seams of the coat and lining separately, then gather the head of the sleeve and sew the coat part of the sleeve into the armhole. The coat and lining at the armhole are either basted or pinned together before sewing in the sleeve.

Now sew a gathering row around the lining sleeve top and clip to the seam in two or three places, especially at the under part of the sleeve. Fold the top of the sleeve lining under at the gathering stitch row and hand sew in place, covering the coat-bodice sleeve joining seam.

Sew the gathered skirt to the coat bodice only, then turn the bottom edge of the bodice lining under and hand stitch in place covering the raw edges.

An edging of lace is hand sewn around the collar and behind the point trims.

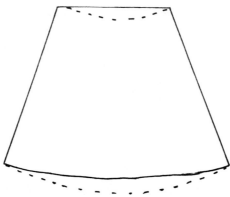

The front side skirt showing the curve to cut to make the skirt hang more evenly, even though it is gathered.

If you desire any applique trim or embroidery on the coat fronts and cape, it's best to apply that trim before the coat and lining are sewn together. The making of the bonnet is described in Chapter 6.

A lovely coat for a toddler is one with a yoke and front panel. The front yoke and panel are cut double on the fold so that one-half is the outside yoke and panel, and the other half serves as facing and part of the lining for the front of the coat.

When making this coat pattern, make the front pattern with an A-line skirt and allow the lapover at the front. Don't worry if the bottom of the skirt pokes out because we will correct that with a dart on the bottom of the bodice.

Draw on the pattern a waistline slightly above the natural waist and then draw, parallel to the front, a straight line for a panel.

Cut away the skirt part created when the bodice and panel were drawn, and split it in several pieces to enlarge the skirt and allow for the gathers.

Remember to allow the seams on the bodice-panel piece as well as the skirt. Fit the bodice, and if a dart under the bust is needed, add extra at the side seam so the bodice will fit. You may not need any extra because of the A-line cut, but be aware that if you do, you add it at the side seam.

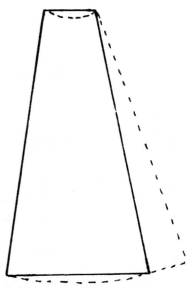

The panel has a slight flare. To give it more flare, add to to the side from the waistline out down to the bottom.

Generally, coats need to have extra allowed for ease of fit over the other clothing so keep that in mind when drawing a pattern. I can't tell you how much to ease because there are so many doll sizes and shapes.

The back of this coat has a gathered skirt. If you wish to pleat the skirt, 2-3 pleats on each side would match the front

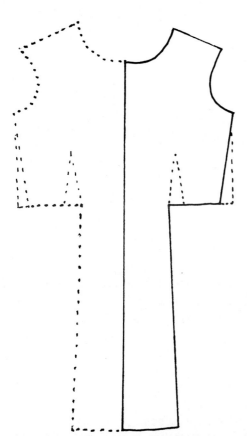

The front of a coat with a panel down the front. An extention is added to the side of the bodice to replace the material used in the dart.

A happy duo in coats made from the same pattern.

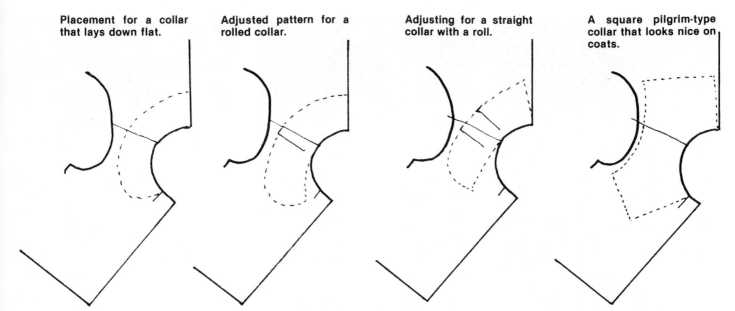

Placement for a collar that lays down flat.

Adjusted pattern for a rolled collar.

Adjusting for a straight collar with a roll.

A square pilgrim-type collar that looks nice on coats.

pleats by not having all the pleats going one way. Also, a gored skirt or a flared skirt could be used.

To make a flared skirt for the front, cut an A-line pattern with the waist or top the same size as the bodice waist. To give it a nice flare, scoop out the top of the skirt in a saucer shape or quarter-moon shape and see how pretty it will flare. Do the same with the back. This type of cut will bring part of the fullness to the center of each front instead of having all the flared fullness on the sides. This cut is good even when the skirt is gathered because you can have plenty of fullness without too much bulk around the waist.

Just a word or two about a fine fitting collar that will lay without showing the under collar. I usually cut the collar facing the same size as the top collar and sew them as if they were one piece but I cut the under collar smaller. Again, I can't tell you exactly how much smaller because of the different sizes, but try 1/8" all the way around for starters. Be sure to put matching marks or outward notches on the top and under collar patterns before cutting out the fabric. Then, when they are put togeth-

er, even though the under collar is smaller, you can match the notches and have a balanced collar.

After sewing around the collar, clip it in several places and turn right side out. On some heavier materials, I cut away one of the seams almost to the seam line and then clip the other for less ridge around the collar. Then again, depending on the material, I top stitch close to the seam on the right side of the under-collar with the seams turned so I catch them in the stitch, and then trim away any excess inside seams.

Remember to have the neck seams even on the collar and undercollar, even though you think the underside is pulling. Try it and see if it doesn't work well that way. Cuffs, pocket flaps and other additions to coats can be sewn in a like manner and they will look well-tailored and lay nicely.

The princess coat is made using your princess dress pattern, enlarged for fit, and a front lap allowed. A pretty princess coat would be one with an opening and buttons down the left front side panel at the seam.

Jackets are made the same way as coats, with linings, sleeves, collars, etc., only shorter, and some can have a peplum or ruffle around the waist. A peplum is a very short skirt, usually flared, but can be gathered or pleated or just hanging straight with open seams from the waist down, and edged in braid.

A bolero is a short jacket that ends above the waistline and usually doesn't have sleeves. The dress or blouse under the bolero will have beautiful sleeves, however. The bolero can have a short or three-quarter sleeve, allowing the blouse sleeve to show part-way, or even a lace ruffle on the bolero sleeve could serve as the complete sleeve. The bolero usually has a rounded front and doesn't close at the neck, but it can have a square front and a neck closing.

This closing is pretty when made of braid in what is called a frog. The hole and the button are of braid and each has a pattern of braid attached. Many oriental pieces of clothing use this type of closure.

If you're wondering how to trim your coat with fur, see Chapter 9.

Paper towel sleeves are pinned into the armholes to decide whether we want them straight or with fullness. The buttons are pinned to the front to decide on placement.

Another row of buttons has been pinned to the coat. To help decide the sleeve style, some trim has been added.

Trim is added to the collar area to determine the collar style.

Will it look better with more trim on the back?

A beautiful dressy coat.

The back of the dressy coat.

Chapter 6

Headwear—Bonnets, Caps and Hats

There was a time when people didn't venture outside unless they had a covering on their head, and the many types and style of headgear would fill more than one book.

We will deal with just enough that our dolls will be well-dressed and feel that their costumes are complete.

Baby bonnets can be simple or

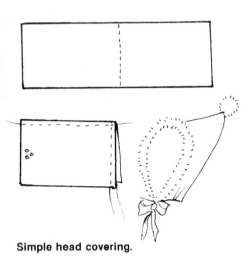

Simple head covering.

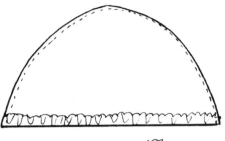

A very simple bonnet that can be made fancy with more trimming.

elaborate.

The simple one can be made of a rectangle piece of fabric long enough to fit around the baby's face and deep enough to come together at the back of her head. Sew a trim on one side of the rectangle piece and fold the material together lengthwise and stitch the back together. Sew a length of ribbon to bind the neck area and hold in any extra with tucks. Extend the ribbon for ties and turn the bonnet right side out. There will be a peak that can be trimmed with a tassel, a pom-pom or folded back and fastened down with a button for trim.

Another simple bonnet for a baby doll can be made from the same material as the dress or coat. Measure the doll over its head from below the ear on one side to below the ear on the

other. If the ear is high on the head, measure to where the side of the face joins the neck. Draw this line on a piece of paper and measure from the front center of the head over the crown to the nape of the neck. Draw this line perpendicular from the center of the first line and draw a half-circle from one end of the first line to the top of the second line

An attractive baby doll bonnet.

A "U" shaped piece in the back of the bonnet.

back down to the other end of the first line.

This simple bonnet has the rounded part gathered to fit the neck and can be trimmed in the front with a ruffle and lace.

Another style is a straight band of material over the head from ear area to ear area with an inset piece at the back, the shape of an upside-down U, that can have the open end pinched together a little if needed for a good fitting U.

This bonnet looks nice with gathered lace around the U and two rows across the front. A

A crocheted bonnet.

Another crocheted bonnet in the knot stitch.

The same type of doily shaped into a hat.

A crocheted doily made into a head covering.

Crocheted doily hat.

Doily stiffened with sugar water.

Back view.

Front view.

A fancy bonnet, front view.

Back view.

lace-edged ruffle can make it more elaborate. Again, try making a narrow band for the front piece and gathering a length of material between the front band and the inset at the back with gathered lace or a lace-edged ruffle between the first and second section of the bonnet. The silk bonnet that completes the costume on our K&R#122 is made in this style and, instead of a ruffle, has a poke that lays back over the front of the bonnet and is decorated with applique and trimmed in the same style as the coat.

Older dolls wear bonnets also, but they have pokes (a brim-like extension rounded to fit around the face) and are usually quite elaborate. The main body part of the bonnet is made with the U, a gathered stripe and a band. A poke over the face completes the bonnet and will need stiffening for it to hold its shape. I have used buckram, cardboard, plastic and multi-stitched rows on several layers of material.

If you want to add style, cut the gathered section wider through the center and eliminate the gathers down the straight side of the U.

Often, ribbons, flowers and feathers adorn these bonnets.

Another lovely bonnet can be made from a lace circle either crocheted with a simple stitch or an actual doily. A ribbon laced near the edge to fit the head and streamers with bows or ribbon rosettes over the ears, will complete this bonnet. The lace circle will also make a mop or beret-type of head covering. Small doilies, saturated with heavy sugar water and shaped over a cup or other shape with the edge pressed flat to a surface, will, when dry, make a lovely hat for a smaller doll.

I find buckram excellent for inner facing for the purpose of shape or body. I cut it the exact

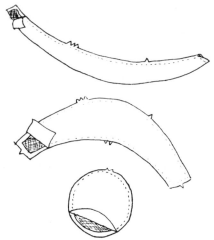

These diagrams show plastic or buckram inner lining that is enclosed within the hat and lining without being sewn in the seams.

size needed without a seam allowance and stitch it between two layers of the hat material. When the hat pieces are sewn together, you will have shape without bulk at the seams. For example: if I want a hat with a short crown, a flat top and a brim, I will make it with the enclosed buckram on the top and crown. The outside edge of the brim will not have a seam allowance but will be flush with the buckram and finished with a binding. If you want the brim to turn up slightly all around, pull the binding as you sew it to the brim. This will draw the brim in and cause it to turn up slightly.

Wire can be used to shape brims by enclosing wrapped milliners wire in the brims. There are several weights so use the one that works well with the material used and the style wanted. Use two strands of wire if one isn' strong enough.

Wire can be used to make shapes for lace or flower-covered bridal headpieces. A horsehair tubing can be purchased from a millinery supply house, which slips over the wire and provides a base on which to sew the lace or flowers. If you wish, lace can be glued to the wrapped wire but be sure the wire is wrapped in white if the lace is white.

The mop or dust cap is used for nightcaps, children's doll head covers and even fancy hats for older dolls. The basic pattern for a mop cap is a circle. An easy way to draw a circle is to make a loop at one end of a piece of string, decide on the size of the circle and make another loop in the string at the other end exactly half the size of the circle.

Place your pattern paper over a surface that you can put a thumb tack in, as one end of the string has a thumb tack to hold it in the center of the paper. Do not push the tack in all the way; let the string move freely. Place a pencil or pen point in the other loop and, holding the pen perpendicular, draw the circle with the string as the guide.

If you want a self-material ruffle, add the ruffle size. If the ruffle is to be lace or eyelet, no extra is needed. You will need to allow a casing for the elastic or drawstring needed to fit the cap around the doll's head.

This circle can be used for several other caps or hats. Sew the circle to a band that fits the

This is one version of a dust or mop cap.

One version of dust cap.

This tam is made by sewing the cutout darts.

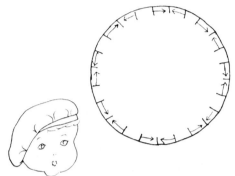
This tam is made by folding in box pleats and sewing the circle to a band.

A half bonnet using a poke and a band only.

doll's head and you have a boy's head covering. Add a small poke for a little older boy doll; or add a brim all around and you will have a lovely hat for any doll. Sometimes the brim can be a double straight or bias piece of the same material pleated or gathered. The possibilities are endless.

A boy's cap.

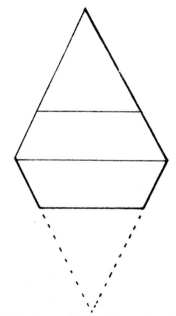
This is the A on a pattern for a pieced tam.

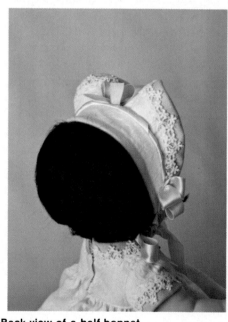
Back view of a half-bonnet.

Another head covering is the boy's cap made with four or more pieces in the crown part and a visor-type brim across the front. This style can be adapted to a tam by cutting the pieces in an A shape on one side and extending the piece from the ends of the A legs in a reverse A shape ending at the crossbar of the A.

This tam is best when made with six or more sections. The total measurement of the crossbars will be the measurement around the doll's head.

Another tam can be made with two circles, one being doughnut shaped with the hole the size of the head's circumference.

The tam can also be made using a straight piece of fabric three times the measurement around the head and half the width of the desired finished size from one ear to the other. Allow for an elastic casing and gathering

rows.

To make this type, sew the two ends together and hem the casing. Sew the gathering rows on the other side and pull the threads tight as possible.

Sometimes, depending on the fabric, you cannot pull the threads tight enough to close the opening and you will have a hole. This hole can be covered with a circle of self-material and a pom-pom, or you can hand stitch the hole together from the wrong side. A tassel or two, a

A stitched brim hat.

Fancy poke bonnet, front view.

Shaped with cardboard, back view.

A character hat.

Charming baby bonnet.

Baby bonnet with ruffle.

button or a loop of self-material can also be used for trim.

Commercial doll hats come in many styles and sizes, and most of them need trimming. Flowers and ribbons look nice and some brims look more finished if you bind them with material or ribbon. Even lace can be used for this purpose.

These hats make good foundations when you want a fabric-covered hat.

An easy, quick way to cover a hat with a brim is to cut a length of fabric the measurement around the outside of the brim

A fancy bonnet with knotted ribbon rosettes.

Side view.

Covered commercial hat with poke.

Back view.

Cloth covered straw hat.

Ribbon trimmed straw poke.

Back view.

Notice trim at poke edge.

and twice the depth of the brim plus seams. After sewing the ends together, stitch a gathering row on each side of the band and place the center around the edge of the brim with one gathered side to the underside and one on the top side. Pull the gathering threads to fit and hand stitch in place at the bend of the brim. Make a circle of material large enough to fit over the entire crown and stitch a gathering line around it. Hand stitch it in place and cover the raw edges with lace, ribbon or a band of self-material gathered through the center.

Try cutting the band for the brim and the trim around the crown on the bias. Often this gives a softer look. Sometimes it's necessary to use the fabric double so the weave of the commercial hat doesn't show through the fabric used to cover it.

A special hat can be made of felt or a man's old hat. This felt will need to be wet molded over a shape and dried.

One way for a doll to have a head covering to complete her costume but still show her beautiful hair is to sew a poke to a band, attach ribbons at each end of the band and tie under chin.

Chapter 7

Dressing the Male Doll

Let's dress the baby boy first in a cute romper suit.

By now you can draw or draft a pant pattern and a dress pattern. So for a romper or coverall, we put the two together at the waist and can make any kind of romper we want to.

One cute little suit can have a

A romper suit.

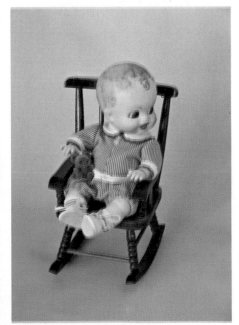

Another style of romper suit.

yoke that is not pieced but is a bodice and the pant part of the rompers is pierced in the center.

You can see that there must be a center seam for the pants to fit nicely but you can do whatever you wish with the top. You can have it open in the front on the shoulder, down the back or off center in the front. But, if you want it with a yoke, first make a half pattern (one side only) and mark the yoke where you want it. Cut off the yoke and allow the seams. The yoke will be cut with the center front on a fold. The rest of the romper front will be cut in two pieces. Always mark the grain of the fabric on each pattern piece. Boy dolls need underwear too and, depending on the doll's size, you can make briefs from a child's sock. Boxer shorts are fine for the older type male doll.

The Katzenjammers are attired as drawn by the artist, one with an eyelet trimmed blouse, opened in the back and a black bolero jacket. The other has a regular boy-type shirt with a bow tie. No instructions needed here, except the dolls had slender hips so the pants slip on without an opening or elastic at the waist. The eyelet collar is a straight piece of eyelet eased slightly to roll.

The baby doll dressed in satin and velvet has a lined jacket and pants. They are velvet. The

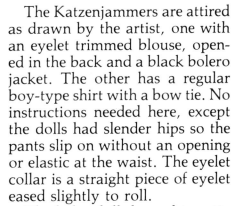

Briefs made from an anklet.

A character costume. The square dancer.

Back view of suit.

blouse is satin. Most materials with a nap need to be cut with all of the pieces laying the same way but this piece of velvet was the exception. Because the nap stands up straight and doesn't lean to one side, I was able to save material in the cutting.

To make the lined jacket edges lay well, I used the continuous cross stitch close to the edge on the lining, the same on the pants. The pants do not have a waist-

A character costume. Charlie.

Charlie's shirt.

Grooms' shirt. Notice the tucked front and the collar for an ascot tie.

band but they do have elastic across the back. To do this, I stitched the pants and the lining separately. I then placed the right side of the pants and the right side of the lining together at the top and stitched them together around the top. I wanted elastic across the back only so I put the pants on the doll and marked the sides, then I pinned the elastic to one side and stretched it around the back to the other marked side and cut that amount of elastic. The pants are still wrong side out, so sew the elastic at the sides on the seam part. Now turn the pants right side out and hand stitch a casing across the back part only, enclosing the elastic.

Sew the crotches separately. To finish the legs, turn the bottom of the velvet under and baste around the edge. Because the leg is curved, you will need to clip the bottom of the leg through the center part of the curve in a place or two. Baste around the bottom of the lining as well and join them together with the continuous cross stitch.

The collar on this outfit is on the shirt but the cuffs are sewn to the bolero or jacket sleeves and the blouse is sleeveless. This not only looks nice but is also less bulky on the arm.

Knit material makes fine suits for boy dolls. They can have the antique look by trimming them with silk. An excellent source for knits is the local thrift store. Sometimes you find a sweater that is exactly what you want, or a sweater can trigger an idea that will be super.

The man doll's clothing can really bring out your tailoring talent and, if you don't have that talent, here are a few things to do that will make people think you do.

Get the pressing board out including the wooden pressing arm and press all of the material

A velvet suit completely lined.

A boy's suit also completely lined.

Back view of suit.

—42—

before cutting. This wooden pressing arm is described in Chapter 14.

Let's tailor a man doll's suit. Our doll is marked for measuring and, as the poor fellow doesn't like standing around without anything on, let's make him some shorts. Measure, draw and cut his shorts using the information in Chapter 2. Allow enough fold back in front to make a simulated fly. Sew a band of elastic either covered or uncovered at the waist.

Notice this doll's legs do not have any joints as I do not intend for him to sit and I want the pant legs to have an unbroken look. Also, note his seat and the fact that his legs are straight down from his tummy. This tells us that most of the crotch will need to be on the back part of the pants.

After making the pattern, cut it first in paper towel material or muslin and try it for fit. You do want the inseam half-way inside his leg and the outseam half-way down the outside of his leg.

Because of the back side being larger, you may need to make the back leg a little wider than the front leg. To avoid waist bulk and since he will be wearing his coat all the time, we will not have a waistband and loops for a belt. The top will either be faced

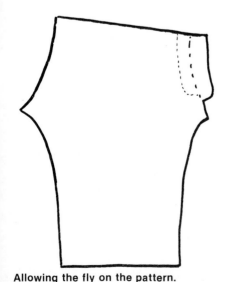
Allowing the fly on the pattern.

with lining or the fabric extended long enough for it to be the facing. If you have a fine enough zipper, use it in the fly. If not, the front can be closed with snaps.

It's best to allow for the fly in the pattern as the extra seam needed to sew a piece on for the fly would add unneeded bulk. To make side pockets on the slant, cut two extra patterns of the top part of the front pants pattern. You will have the pant front pattern and the two extra.

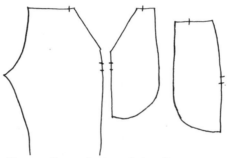
Diagram for a slant pocket pattern.

From the pant front pattern cut off the side top corner on a long slant for the pocket opening. You determine the size. Now place the pant pattern on the other two short patterns so they match at the side and top, pin to hold. Cut the first short piece to match the pocket on the pant pattern. Lift the top pattern off and draw the pocket deepness on the top pattern and cut the two short pieces the same along the rounded mark of deepness. One piece will be the pocket facing and the other will be the back of the pocket and the top side corner of the pants.

Sew the back seam and the darts in the back. Sew the side seams, catching the side of the pocket in as well. Press all seams open. If the material is wool, open the seams and dip your finger into a bowl of water and rub your finger along the inside of the seam and press the seam. After you have sewn the inseams and crotch, use the long-armed

pressing board to open and press those seams.

If you were making tuxedo pants, a stripe of satin or ribbon would either be stitched in the side seam or top stitched to the side seam. Hem the legs by hand and press. Fold over the top for a facing or sew on a facing and finish the edge by turning under or overcasting. Catch the facing to the pants at the seams and darts. Turn the pants right side out and match the side seam to the inseam of each leg and press in the creases. They should be sharp so press with a double layer of a damp man's handkerchief. They do make nice pressing cloths for small clothing.

Sometimes you can skip some of the parts and still achieve the total look. For example, my modern-day "Blue Boy" doesn't have any pockets at all as they don't show. However, he does have his pants open up the back seam so the post part of the doll stand can slip up under the pant's waist and shirt to the shoulder plate (reference Chapter 1).

Our dear fellow has underwear and pants so let's outfit him in a regular shirt with a collar and cuffs, back yoke and button front.

Check out a man's shirt and notice the collar generally has two sections, a neck band and a collar. Also the yoke is part in the front and part in the back. So let's make a pattern. It may seem complicated but it really isn't. Just make a back and front basic pattern in paper that fits well around the neck, pin together the shoulder seams. Now draw on the yoke. Cut along the lines and make the yoke final pattern by tracing around the yoke and adding the seams. Make a notch mark at the shoulder seam spot so you will know where to sew the top center of the sleeve. Make the final front pattern by allowing seams, including a fold back for buttons on the right side and a wider fold over to the front for the buttonhole panel.

If there is a right and wrong side to your shirt material, you will need to cut a separate panel. It's nice to put a small tuck or gathered area at the center back or on each back shoulder in the back part of the shirt. To allow for this in the final pattern, lay the draft center back on the fold. Keeping the bottom area even with the folded edge, slide the top area over; leave a space between the folded edge and the center back of the draft back pattern. Make this space the size you want the tucks. Remember to allow for seams on the final pattern.

Draw and cut the sleeve pattern allowing for a cuff and some fullness. The collar band fits the neck, including the lap needed to button the shirt. It is rounded at the front top so the shirt collar will come together when the shirt and collar band are lapped over and buttoned. The finished collar is exactly the neck size and parts at the front to make room for the tie.

Notice how the sleeve placket

Tailored shirt and pants.

is made and where it is placed on a regular shirt and do the dolls the same. The collar and cuffs are inner lined. I use the same shirt material for inner lining.

The shirt collar needs a little roll so I place the collar under the pressure foot with the top collar down. The natural action of the feed dog on the machine will pull the under layer for that little extra fullness needed on the top collar to help it roll nicely. By roll, I mean to turn back and lay nicely without a tendency to draw up or pull.

Clip the collar corner excess material on a slanted cut toward the corner on each side. As there are three layers, turn the collar right side out so the bottom piece will be on the top. Work the seam out to the edge between your fingers and pin or press so the collar can be top stitched.

After top stitching, place the raw edge of the collar between the neckband material at each end. Stitch, clip and turn. The neck band is three layers too, so sew two layers to the shirt neck after the yoke and fronts are finished and top stitch the third down to cover the stitching.

Put a pocket on the shirt if you wish.

Now the jacket. We can make a nice sport jacket to complement the shirt and trousers of another material, or a suit jacket of the same material as the pants. One difference will be in the stitching on the lapel. The suit coat looks nice if the collar and lapel are stitched on the very edge but we can take liberties with the sport jacket by machine stitching in ¼" and using a contrasting color thread or by hand stitching in various size stitches or by using a picking stitch which looks nice on a plain material.

The picking stitch is made with buttonhole twist or similar thread and only a dot shows on the top at evenly spaced intervals.

A sport coat can have a different back treatment including a yoke, pleats and a belt.

We have an example of a sort of sport jacket in the "Hobo's" coat, and "Charlie" has a character suit jacket. Our "Blue Boy" is in a very formal coat with satin lapels. So perhaps we should complete our "feller's" outfit with a well-tailored suit coat.

The shape of the layers for the shoulder pad. The thickness will depend upon the doll.

To get the coat pattern, make a paper towel pattern of the front and fit it over his clothes, plus a shoulder pad. Make the shoulder pad with horsehair material if you can find any. It's a tailoring material used in men's suits. Take an old coat apart and get some that way. It is usually in the lapel and often down the front. There will be some cotton flannel inside also. If not, outing or diaper flannel will be fine.

Cut a triangle of horsehair cloth that is longer at the base than at the point. It should fit over the shoulder down about 1½" to the front and 1½" to the back with the point within a third of the shoulder length from the neck. For each shoulder pad cut one piece of horsehair fabric that size and the one the same length from shoulder to arm **but ⅛" longer and larger on each side — not the base side.** This pad is for a 16-19" doll. Cut from flannel two the same size as the first horsehair cloth triangle and one the size of the second horsehair triangle. Cut two flannel layers a little smaller than the first flannel triangle and two more smaller still.

Lay the first or smaller

horsehair fabric triangle over the doll's shoulder so it looks like it's in the right place for the coat shoulder. You will want a slightly broad shoulder look. Place a flannel layer, then build up the pad by placing all of the flannel on the pad one at a time, starting with the smallest. Keep the base or area at the armhole even.

Place the second or larger horsehair fabric triangle on last. Pin the pad together along the shorter triangle edges and remove it from the doll's shoulder. Hand stitch the pad where it is pinned, and also put three or four stitches across the base line, but do not pull them tight.

There are other materials you can use for the pad but the horsehair inner lining with flannel works very well. Use more or less layers if you need more or less.

Place the finished shoulder pad on the doll's shoulder and pin it in place. Make the pattern to accommodate the pad.

To get the coat lapel, make one side of the front only. On the paper towel pattern allow about an inch overlap. Pin the pattern to the doll at the seam, the center front and the shoulder line. Check to make sure the coat neck is on the neckline. Fold the overlap back to form a lapel and draw the lapel line. Also draw the overlap line from the waist down and curve the corner of the overlap at the front bottom.

You may want more point or shape to the lapel. If so, tape on more paper and mark the addition. The coat may fit better in the front if there is a small, long dart through the center of the front side.

The back will have a seam down the middle, so some of the shoulder broadness can be at the center back and taper to the waist. Pin and fit the back of the coat in paper towelling. The coat should fit well, yet hang free, so

Using the "U" method to diagram the underarm piece of a two-piece sleeve.

don't make it too tight or fitted at the waist.

Make a paper collar to fit the neckline to the lapel area. This collar is straight across except there will be a **slight** curve where it fits the front part of the neckline to the lapel.

Measure the armseye and divide the measurement into thirds. Draw an undersleeve by drawing a U-shaped line with the left end longer than the other. This U-shaped line should measure 1/3 the armseye measurement. Spread the top ends of the U apart until they are four times as wide as the first U. Check the measurement again and take off any extra but still have one side a little longer than the other; mark the longer line "B" for back. Draw a straight line down from the center of the bottom of the U the length of the underarm.

Decide how wide you want the bottom of the sleeve to be and take 1/3 of that measurement and draw a line across at the bottom of the underarm measurement line with 1/3 of the 1/3 measurement on the back side of the line and the 2/3 of the 1/3 measurement on the front side of the line.

Draw a slightly curved outline from the longer end of the U

to the end of the 1/3 line at the bottom of the undersleeve. Draw a slightly curved in-line on the other side, joining the top of the U to the end of the 2/3 of the 1/3 measurement line. This is your undersleeve without a hem or seams.

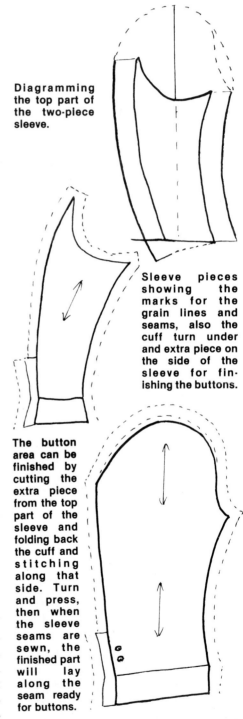

Diagramming the top part of the two-piece sleeve.

Sleeve pieces showing the marks for the grain lines and seams, also the cuff turn under and extra piece on the side of the sleeve for finishing the buttons.

The button area can be finished by cutting the extra piece from the top part of the sleeve and folding back the cuff and stitching along that side. Turn and press, then when the sleeve seams are sewn, the finished part will lay along the seam ready for buttons.

To make the top part of the sleeve, draw a line across the lower part of the paper the 2/3 bottom of the sleeve measurement. Draw up from the center the measurement, on the doll's arm, from the wrist over the edge of the shoulder pad to meet the coat shoulder. Place the underarm pattern over the upper arm lines so the center of the underarm is on the center of the upper arm measurement.

The bottom wrist measurement will extend out on each side. Draw the upper arm lines up, using the length of the wrist line as a guide. Make the back line the same distance from the back line of the under sleeve all the way up to the top of the U. Do the same on the front line. Draw a rounded line to equal ⅔

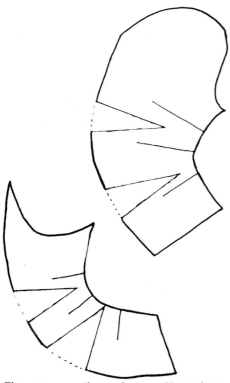

The curves on these sleeve pattern pieces look exaggerated but I used this pattern on a jacket for a doll with curved arms and they looked fine.

of the armseye, from the top of the back line over the top of the center line on the upper sleeve and down to the top of the front upper sleeve line.

If you have any of the ⅔ of the armseye measurement left over after the last line, draw a larger rounded line. If you do not

have enough, draw in the amount needed as it can be adjusted in the top of the sleeve roll. Pin the paper towel pattern on the doll's arm. Check for extra fullness at the arm's curve.

If there is a deep bend in the doll's arm, the pattern can be adjusted with a tuck at the front of the upper sleeve and lower sleeve front seams. After pinning the tuck, release the pins of the back sleeve seam and slit the pattern at the elbow in order for the sleeve to fit a deep arm curve.

Make the final pattern including a pocket flap pattern, and we are ready to cut the garment.

Cut a lapel facing and front lining by drawing a line from the center of the shoulder in a curve about ⅓ of the width across the bottom of the jacket. Make the curve toward the center of the front of the jacket. The lapel part is cut in the suit fabric and the rest in lining. Remember to allow the seams.

Cut the top collar in fabric on the grain and the under collar on the bias. Cut the inner facing for the lapels and collar on the bias.

Before doing any machine sewing, except darts, place the inner facing on the front of the suit and hand stitch to the suit fabric with long and tiny stitches in rows through the lapel area. Do the same with the collar inner facing and the bias under collar. The long stitches will be on the

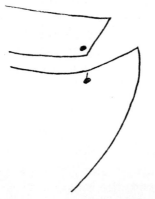

Matching the collar to the neck of the jacket.

inner facing side and the tiny stitches, barely showing, will be on the fabric.

Baste the inner facing to the suit fabric all around the edges. The pocket flaps are sewn next.

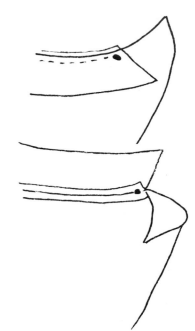

Stitch the right collar to the jacket and sew the other collar to the lining and lapel piece, being sure to match the circles.

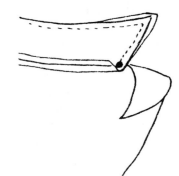

Starting at circle, sew the collars together.

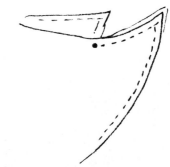

Matching the same circle, sew around the jacket lapel and down the front of the jacket. To make sure you get the circles even, pin through them with a straight pin and have the machine needle down through both parts of the garment right next to the pin before you start to sew.

Sew the front facing to the lining, and the front shoulders to the back shoulders in both the lining and the coat.

Sew the side seams.

Sew the collar with the inner facing to the neckline of the coat with the inner facing and the straight collar to the lining and the lapel neckline. Clip and press the neck seams open.

Now comes the ticklish part. Sew the collars together, being very careful to start and stop exactly where the collars join the lapels. Use a circle mark as a guide and pin together. After sewing, snip off the extra material on the collar where the collars join the lapel and from the corners of the collar.

Sew the lapels together, starting at the exact point where the lapels join the collar and ending along the bottom around the curve to the end of the facing. Clip where needed, including the point, any curves and the area where you started sewing the lapels together.

Using the wooden pressing board, press all of the seams open, including around the collar and lapels. Stitch the collar seams together at the neckline. (See illustration.)

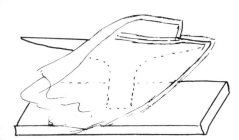

Press the seams flat using the tailoring board. Clip the seams and cut off the excess material at all corners including the corners on the collar at the circle area.

Turn the collar and lapels right side out and machine stitch around their edge as close to the edge as possible, turn, topstitch and sew on the pocket flaps.

For a hand-tailored look, a tiny hand sewn stitch can be substituted. Sew the side seams

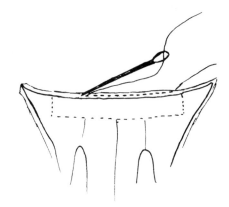

Stitching the collar seams at the neckline.

and the sleeve seams. After pressing them open, cut a 1" wide piece of muslin, long enough to fit across the top part of the sleeve along the seam. It does not have to reach down to the sleeve side seams.

Sew a gathering row of stitches on the top sleeve or from side seam to side seam, exactly on the seam allowance line. Make sure you are sewing through the sleeve and the muslin, which has been placed flush with the edge of the sleeve. One-fourth of an inch of the bias will be in the seam and ¾ will be in the sleeve.

This bias piece gives substance to the sleeve roll. Sew the fabric sleeve into the fabric **only** part of the coat. The lining comes later. Press the top of the sleeve seam **open,** clipping where needed. Turn the lining back up over the collar area and sew the raw edges of the coat, lining and lapel at the neckline together with a basting stitch. This prevents the collar and lapel from shifting.

Place the shoulder pad in the shoulder so it looks nice. It should protrude into the sleeve about the width of the seam. Secure in several places with hand stitching.

Lay back the lapel in the proper fold and pin the coat and lining together along the seam that joins the lapel to the front lining.

Turn the lining back and catch the raw edges to the coat by hand in several places. Usually it can be caught to the shoulder pad, the inner facing, or perhaps the dart. If you need to catch it to the coat fabric itself, try to catch just part of a thread and keep the stitches loose.

Baste the lining armhole and hem the coat with as invisible a stitch as possible. Catch the lining side seam to the coat side seam and stitch the coat lining at the hemline. Sew it to the hem, halfway up the hem so it will not hang down and show below the coat.

Machine stitch around the lining armseye of the sleeve and, after clipping the underarm area, hand stitch the sleeve lining into the armhole covering all the raw edges. Be sure to match the center top and seams.

The suit coat completes the outfit.

Next the coat sleeves are hemmed and the lining stitched in place like the coat lining bottom. Sew tiny buttons on each sleeve on the front side of the back seam. Make one or more buttonholes on the left front of the jacket and close with buttons.

Now all our friend needs is a tie. He can wear a bow tie, or make him one from the instructions given in Chapter 13.

The buttonhole: On sheer material, embroider the buttonhole first and then cut it with sharp pointed scissors or a razor blade. For heavier material such as coats and suits, cut the hole and whip stitch baste around the hole to hold the pieces together. Using single buttonhole twist, hold the garment at the buttonhole area between the thumb and forefinger of the left hand. Place the needle inside and pull through, at the right end bottom side of buttonhole, a stitch the width of the buttonhole stitches.

A hand-embroidered keyhole buttonhole with a bar at one end. Shirts usually have bars at both ends.

Place the needle inside and bring it out close to the first stitch but do not pull it all the way; pick up the thread with the right tonhole and join to the first stitch. A bar can be made at the end of each side, or one side only of the hole by stitching three

stitches in the same place, the width of both sides of the finished buttonhole.

hand, close to the needle eye, and bring the thread down under the needle point from right to left and pull the needle through with the thread forming a knot at the edge of the hole. Continue this stitch around the entire but-

Make a shank on a button by sewing over a pin; after enough stitchs are made, wrap the thread around the stitches between the garment and the button several times after you have removed the pin. Be sure to secure the thread ends.

On suits and coats, it's best to sew the button on using a shank. This is done, after making the first stitch through the button and the material, by slipping a pin under the stitch on top of button. Sew each stitch over the pin.

made, end with the needle between the button and the suit, remove the pin and wrap the thread around the threads between the button and suit several times to form a shank.

One version of a sailor suit on a doll made by Jean Lemmons.

A colorful shirt for the Hobo.

Chapter 8

Trims

SELF MATERIAL TRIMS

The simplicity of a self-trimmed dress can create an outstanding garment providing the dress fits well and the trim is complementary to the style.

That statement could refer to a living person's dress, but it is in reference to doll clothing that the statement was made.

Sometimes, just by draping the

A self trimmed dress.

The difference a touch of lace makes.

fabric, lovely style lines are achieved. Adding a bow of self material in the same or a different color, or the same color in a different material, can be all that the dress will need.

A wide self-material bias can finish the skirt bottom, with narrow bias trim at the neck and cuffs. The addition of jewelry or a flower could complete the dress, and the addition of a hat, a stole or a fur scarf or collar would make it outstanding.

Some bias-trimmed dresses need a little more to make them complete. Try stitching heavy lace over the piecing covering the seam.

Another dress with the addition of lace.

Another way to trim with lace over bias is to hand stitch gathered lace at the seam, this looks very nice around the neck. Sometimes the lace can be sewn on the bias on the wrong side and show at the edge.

Self material ruffles, or any ruffles, can be finished in a number of ways depending on the material. If the material is stiff, like taffeta, pinking the

edge can be sufficient. Another way is to make a tiny hem by machine. The method I use most is to overcast with a zig-zag stitch on my machine.

Several things need to be considered if you are doing a zig hem. First, if you need a long piece of material for ruffles, piece it before hemming. Also, ruffles cut on the bias seem to lay nicer than when cut on the straight of the material. I suggest that you gather a short piece, cut on the bias, and another piece cut straight, before you cut the amount needed for the dress.

Also, to see how the material will hang when gathered, experiment with the various types of hemming to determine which to use. This will also determine how much extra to allow for the hem.

Now back to how I zig overcast. I set the zig stitch on the widest stitch and the length of the stitch is set on a short stitch. You will need to determine the setting according to your machine. After setting your machine, place the end of the ruffle under the pressure foot and start to sew, catching the edge within the zig stitch. After you have sewn an inch or so, you may make any adjustment you need in order to find the nicest stitch combination for that particular hem.

Sometimes I find that the right side of the zig hem looks better if I hem with the wrong side of the material down, and vice versa. It really is a matter of getting to know which stitches work best on your machine. Some hems look nicer with a narrow size setting such as I used on the ruffles made from a lovely piece of silk that I've had for over 24 years.

If you want a heavier edge, zig over the hem a second time. Some ruffles look nice hemmed on each side and gathered through the middle or off center. This works well for pleated ruffles also.

When sewing rows of ruffles on a skirt, allow for an overhang where the ruffles will lap, one over the other, so the stitches don't show. For example, a 6" skirt would not look nice with six rows of 1" ruffles. You would need to make the ruffles about a ½" longer or make 7-8 rows of 1" ruffles.

Ruffles can be gathered by machine with an attachment, or by sewing two rows of long stitches ⅛"-¼" apart along the raw edge and pulling the threads. I suggest two rows as you can control the gathers and the edge of the ruffle much better than when there is only one.

You also save time because having to check to see if the edge of the material is getting caught in the stitches when you are sewing the ruffle on can be time-consuming and frustrating.

Pleating trims a garment nicely and gives a different look from ruffles.

When figuring the amount of material needed for ruffles or pleats, measure the area for the trim and cut your material three times as long plus seams for pleats, and 2½ times as long plus seams for gathers.

Three times the area will give you pleats that lay flush with each other. If you want them deeper, you will need to allow the extra amount.

As a general rule, I pleat my narrow ruffles by folding and stitching with the machine using a long sewing or darning needle; however, this takes practice so I suggest you measure, make marks, and then fold and stitch. I pin the stitched edge to the ironing board and measure and pin the other end of each pleat down by sticking the pin in on a slant. I press the pleats from the stitched end down, slipping out the bot-

tom pins before the iron reaches them. This avoids pressed pin marks.

Pleat boards are on the market and I find they work very well but the pin and iron method works well also.

A folded point of self fabric can make an interesting trim. Use a square piece of material; the size will depend upon how large you want the trim to be.

Fold the square through the middle, fold each folded corner down on an angle to the center of the raw edges. Now you have a triangle with all of the raw edges on one side. Sew along the raw

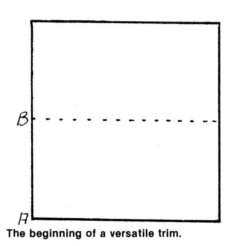
The beginning of a versatile trim.

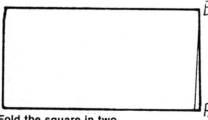
Fold the square in two.

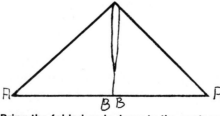
Bring the folded ends down to the center of the raw edge.

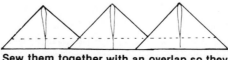
Sew them together with an overlap so they meet at the sewing line.

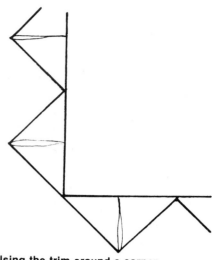
Using the trim around a corner.

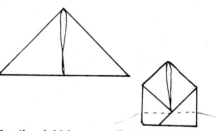
Another fold for a smaller point.

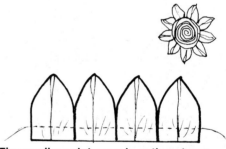
The smaller point sewn in gathered row.

edges to hold the folds in place.

After making as many as you need, stitch them to the garment, overlapping them so there will not be any gaps between them. If they are being used on a corner, arrange them so that one comes just to the corner on each side.

This trim can be used at seams as well as for an edging.

Another self trim extensively used, especially on baby doll clothing, is the tuck. It has been suggested that the original purpose of the tuck was for enlarging the garment as the child grew. The purpose became lost when tucks became so decorative that they became part of the trim on the garment. Often tucks were alternated with inserted bands of lace or eyelet, and even the undergarments became elaborate with tucks.

When planning tucks in a garment, always add double the size of the tuck. For example, if you are having five tucks ¼" wide, you will need to allow **five times** ½", or 2½" extra. Always remember that the material used in tucks is double, and lost material, as it does not add any length.

There are several methods for making even tucks on straight material. One is to measure and mark with pins, then pin together and stitch. Another is to use a gauge when stitching. Pressing in each tuck edge works well, especially if the tuck width matches the pressure foot width,

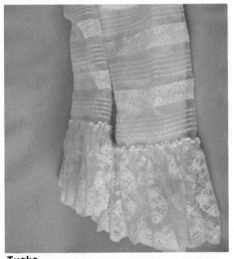

Tucks...

and more tucks.

because you can keep the pressed edge along the foot edge as you sew.

You can also pull a thread and fold the tuck along that line if the material is such that a thread can be pulled out easily. Sometimes you can sew rather than fold along the pulled thread line. At times, tucks follow pattern lines, as in dotted swiss or other dotted material that has dots in an even row.

A pattern of different sized tucks make a nice trim on an apron or pinfore. If the garment is tiny, simulated tucks made with a simple row of machine stitching will be all that is needed to give a nice effect. When doing this, be sure your machine tension is right, otherwise you may get a pulled-thread look.

When using this tuck trim, I usually use a fine zig-zag stitch instead of the single needle stitch; it looks very nice and this type of tucking doesn't require any extra material.

Another way to trim is by binding which is the same as using the bias trim, but it covers the edge of the material on both the right and the wrong side, whereas the bias trim can cover the right side only.

When using binding as a trim, a seam allowance on the garment is not required. Lace or other trims can be used with binding.

Shirring is rows of stitching that are pulled and which form closed-in gathers to allow fullness for skirts, ruffles, sleeves or whatever you plan. Shirring is used frequently on antique doll clothing, especially down the front and along the front of a poke bonnet.

Smocking is another type of trim used most often on children's doll clothing, and creates fullness as does the shirring.

Lace has been used for decorative purposes for hundreds of years and cities have

given their names to a particular lace from their region. Some well-known laces such as Chantilly and Alencon are from France. There is a Venetian lace, beautiful laces from Brussels, Cluny lace, and the ever popular Narrow Val lace used by so many doll makers to enhance the small garments.

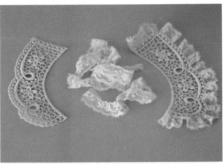

A combination of two laces.

Lace adds a touch of elegance to any garment. Some dresses are completely made of lace and some need only a touch. It is important to use the right lace. A sheer, dainty lace may look out of place on a heavy garment when used alone but when used with a heavy lace in the right combination the result can be enchanting, so don't be afraid to experiment.

Sometimes lace used with another trim will make both trims more interesting. If your lace is droopy, you can back it with a piece of tulle and sew them both as one. Sometimes all it needs is a little spray starch.

It is generally suggested that hand sewing lace to a garment is often the better way. This may be true, but when I am using over 40 yards of lace on a baby doll outfit, I have neither the time nor the inclination to sew it on by hand. In the chapter on baby doll clothes, I tell you how I sew it on by machine and make it look nice. For tiny garments, I love to hand sew the lace with tiny whip stitches.

I always check the lace and press out any wrinkles. If I'm using a narrow lace with picots (loops), I hold the straight edge down with a piece of cardboard cut about 2" times six or eight inches. The cardboard on which rickrack or bias tape is wrapped works very well. I press over the cardboard and lace out to the edge. Sometimes the lace will press without using the cardboard to hold it in place.

When hand sewing gathered lace to a garment, there are several methods you can use. One is to pull the heavy thread, usually found in cotton laces, along the straight edge, and placing the right side of the lace to the right side of the garment, whip stitch the two edges together spacing the gathers evenly. If the lace doesn't have a heavy thread, you can sew a row of machine stitches close to the straight edge and, after whip stitching the lace to the garment, remove the machine-stitched gathering thread.

Another method that works very well and gives nice even gathers, is the gather-as-you go way. Lay the garment material right side up over your index finger on your left hand and hold it with your thumb. This is for people who sew with the needle in their right hand. For people using the left hand just reverse the process. Place the straight edge of the lace along the edge of the garment with the right side of the lace down. Do not knot your thread. Now, slip the needle along your index finger up close to the edge and through the garment material and the lace, leaving about 1" of thread.

Fold the thread end forward along the stitching line and take another whip stitch over the material, lace and thread. Now take a stitch in the lace. Alternate stitches, with one stitch in lace only, then one stitch in the material and the lace, until finished. Catch the thread each

time you sew the material and lace until the inch of thread is covered. This eliminates an unsightly knot.

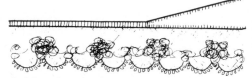

Cutting the ladder rungs on synthetic fiber lace before stitching to the garment.

A dress made of ribbon.

If more fullness is desired in the lace, take two stitches in the lace to one in the material and lace.

Remember to allow extra gathers at any corners. The right side of the lace will have a raised look. Often laces will have a thread or cord outlining the pattern on the right side. For this reason, lace should be pressed on the wrong side.

If you are sewing straight lace around a curve, it helps if you press the lace in a curve first. It also helps to curve the lace if you can pull a thread and gather slightly to fit the curve.

It seems that ribbon goes with lace, and some laces are made with holes through which ribbon can be threaded. A similar effect can be had simply by placing ribbon behind the holes and it will show through.

Ribbon threaded through lace and sewn under it to look like it is threaded.

Ribbon is very versatile and can be the only trim some garments need. A row or two stitched on an underslip to show through a sheer skirt can give a delicate suggestion of color to the garment. Rows of multi-colored ribbons can create a beautiful trim.

Knots tied in ribbon before making a rosette make the rosette more interesting. To make a knotted rosette, tie knots at equal intervals in a length of ribbon. If the ribbon is satin on one side only, tie the knots so the satin shows on both sides of the finished knot. The distance between the number of knots will depend on the size of the ribbon and the fullness of the rosette desired. A safe rule to follow is the narrower the ribbon, the closer the knots.

After you have tied the determined number of knots (or if you aren't sure how large you want the rosette to be, tie a few knots and then tie any additional knots as you make the rosette), hand sew at an even distance between the first two knots with a running stitch and pull the stitches tight. Sew in place several times to secure the gathered stitches.

Without cutting the thread, sew a running stitch the same distance down from the first knot that you stitched between the first and second knot. Pull this stitching into gathers and catch to the first gathering. Sew between the remaining knots and secure at the gathers until you have the size rosette you want.

If the rosette is to be used over the ear area of a bonnet, allow for the tie by leaving the tie length attached to the rosette. If you want two streamers to fall from the rosette, they can be allowed for before tying knots in the ribbon length or they can be separate from the rosette and sewn to the back of the rosette when it is finished.

Another attractive rosette can be made in any size according to the ribbon width. Mark one edge of a piece of ribbon with equal distances between the marks. Alternate the marks on the opposite edge by keeping them equal but having the marks halfway between the first marks.

How to stitch ribbon or folded material to make a gathered trim or rosettes.

Hand stitch from one mark through the ribbon to the opposite mark until you have stitched to all the marks. I usually sew over the edge and down the next line to the mark so the edges will be held in. Pull the threads tightly and arrange the resulting puffs into a rosette. One edge of the puffs will be for the center and the other edge of the puffs will make petals.

The gathered trim can have pinked edges, hemmed edges, raw bias edges or zig hemmed edges.

One way to pleat material or ribbon for insertion.

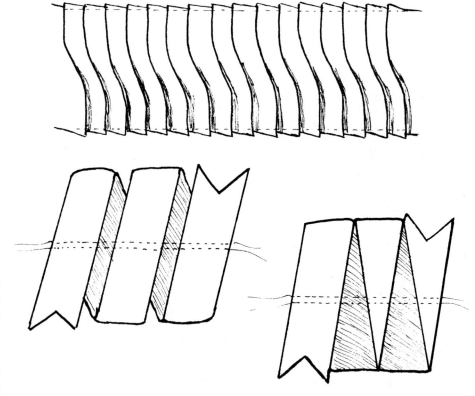

This trim is especially nice on French doll shoes when made of a narrow ribbon. A wider ribbon rosette made this way is lovely over the ear of a crocheted baby doll bonnet. If you gather the ribbon slightly, you will have a lovely trim to use on dresses as an edging. Ribbon can also be gathered and pleated at both

—53—

edges and used for edging or trim.

If you pleat one side of the ribbon in one direction and the other side in the opposite direction, you will have a very interesting trim. Sometimes a complete garment can be made from ribbon.

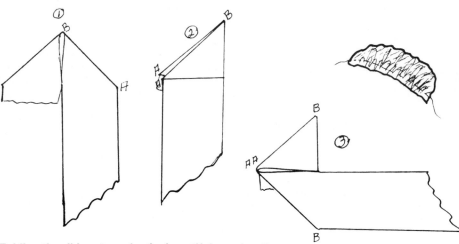

Folding the ribbon to make the beautiful passion flower rosette.

Pleated silk ribbon on a silk ribbon skirt. Notice her shirred blouse.

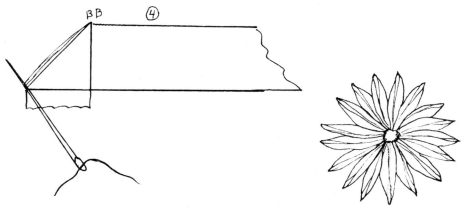

After each fold to the top, catch the point with thread so when all the points are folded they will be joined; catch the points to the garment with a tiny stitch or a bead.

Hair bows.

Bows and more bows — bows in a row — bows in the hair.

When making a bouffant bow for the hair, a taffeta ribbon works very well because you don't have to worry about keeping the satin side out.

Just determine the bow size and lay the ribbon in layers the desired size. In days gone by one

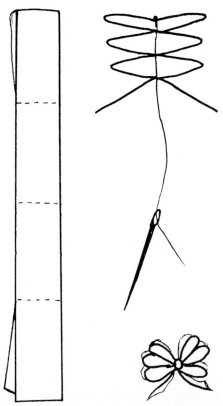

Another way to make a bow.

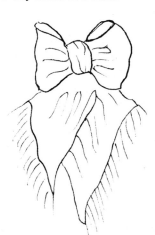

Cloth bows with fringe are very decorative.

could use a special hair clamp with a special holder that the folded ribbon was placed in after pinching it together through the center. This clamp was used in place of the knot. I find when making this type of bow if the ribbon is layered in a staggered pattern the bow will look very nice.

If you are using a ribbon with satin on one side, the method is different. First you determine the bow size and number of loops. If the bow is to be 4" and have six loops (three on each side) plus two ends, your ribbon will need to be 32" long. The completed bow has 2" wide loops. Each loop is double, so figure 4" per loop. There will be six loops — a total of 24". When determining the amount of ribbon to purchase, allow 2½" for each end. Allow ½" for each loop for the knot area. You need a total of 34".

The knot is cut separately and requires about 2". Crease in the center and fold the ribbon double at the crease.

Measure 4½" down from the crease and sew across at the mark from selvage to selvage, mark down another 4½" and sew. Repeat one more time. Open each loop and layer the ribbon matching each row of stitching upon the other. Match the fold crease to the stitching. The ends will each be to one side.

Tack the bow together at the seams and wrap the piece of knot ribbon around and stitch on the underside. The knot will look nice if you pleat one end of the knot ribbon and sew it to the underside of the bow. Bring the ribbon up over the top of the bow and pleat the other knot ribbon end in the opposite direction, fold under the excess and stitch down, covering the first knot stitching. You may have a little too much knot ribbon so cut off the unneeded part.

Slip a bobby pin through the underside of the knot to hold the bow on the doll's head, or pin it to the wig with two pins near the knot area, pinned at different angles.

This same method can be used for a simple two loop bow (one on each side of knot) or a tailored bow without any ribbon ends to show.

To tie a single bow so the satin side will show on both the loops and the ends is not difficult but does require both the right and left hand and several fingers.

To determine the amount of ribbon needed, first decide on the bow size. Let's make a 4" bow with 3" angled ends, out of 1" wide ribbon. (Actually the ribbon will be a little under 1" — that's usually the way it comes.)

Okay, the bow is to be 4" and the loops are double, so start with 8". The ends are to be 3", so add 6" more. As ends are to be mitered (cut on an angle), allow 1" extra for each end. You now have 16" of ribbon — but, we must not forget the knot which will use about 2". So, for a 4" bow of 1" ribbon, we will need 18".

METHOD TO TIE BOW

Fold the ribbon, with the satin side out, on the mark determined by the bow and end sizes. This bow will have 3" ends plus the inch for mitering, plus one loop which is 2" (½ of the 4" bow). Therefore, make the fold 6" from end #1, (end #1 will be the end at your right hand when the ribbon is laying on a surface in front of you, with the satin side up) with the satin side out and the longer piece to the back.

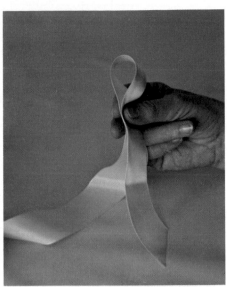

2. Lay the middle finger below the index finger to hold the ribbon.

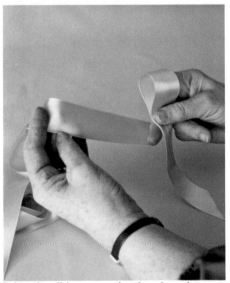

Bring the ribbon over the thumb and across the back.

1. Pinch a loop with the satin side out.

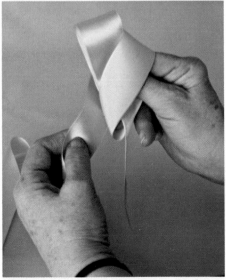

With the wrong side showing to the front.

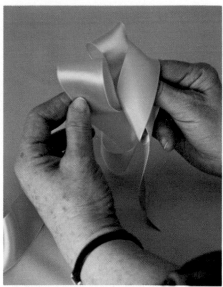

5. Pinch another loop with the satin side out.

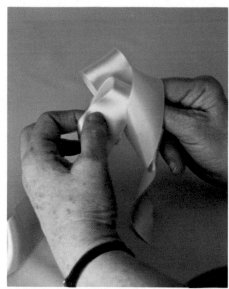

6. Slip the loop through the space made by Step 3 & 4.

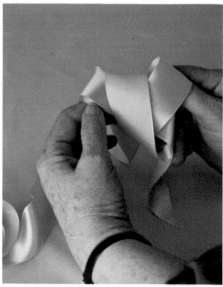

7. Slide the thumb up...

8. into the loops and hold...

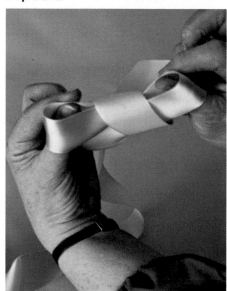

9. with index fingers.

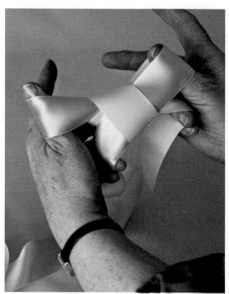

10. Grasp the ends between the ring and little fingers and hold securely.

11. Manipulate into a bow by pulling all parts...

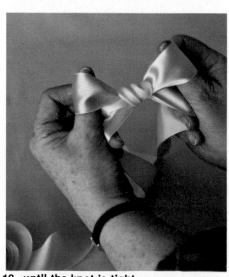

12. until the knot is tight.

13. Cut both ends off evenly and you have a bow with the satin showing to the front.

Now measure down from the fold 2″ (½ the bow size) and pinch the ribbon between the right thumb and index finger. Place your right middle finger on the ribbon just below the thumb and index finger. It should protrude out from the index finger as it will be used to wrap the ribbon around to form the knot. Still pinching the ribbon in your right hand, use your left hand to bring the long end of the ribbon behind the end of the right middle finger. You will see the ribbon's satin side

Now, with the left hand, lay the ribbon over the front of the ribbon at the pinched area, the satin side will be under at this point. Bring the ribbon around the back of the loop in the right hand, slip it down so the index finger is holding it also, and with the ribbon folded double, use the left hand to slip a loop down through the opening formed by the wrong side of the ribbon. Keep the loop short.

Here's the tricky part. Slip your thumbs up into the **loops** from the bottom of the loops and grasp the back part of the loops with the thumbs and index fingers. Hold on to the loops while grasping the ends near the loops between your middle and fourth fingers, one end to each hand. Be sure the ends have the satin side facing you and the middle finger is behind the ribbon and the fourth finger in front. Gently pull

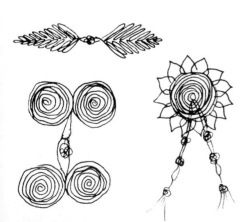

Braids and cords can be rolled into lovely designs for trim as well as closures.

from the back of the loops with your thumb and index finger at the same time. Pull on the ends carefully until the knot tightens and the loops are the same size, with the ends hanging down at a nice angle. Miter the ends so the point is to the inside of the bow and there you have it.

No — well, try again. It really works — it just takes practice. The bow will be all satin except the knot.

There are a great number of cords and braids on the market today that will look lovely when used for trim just as they are; for scrolls, loops, bands or rows; as

The art of applique enhances many garments.

Cloth roses.

Pearls on lace.

The rick rack braid trim.

covering for seams, and rolled for closures. Also, you can use them in combination with other braids or trims.

Soutach braid is a simple braid that can turn elegant when sewn in a pattern to decorate coats and jackets, or when braided and used for edges, etc. Use one color or three colors to braid, for example, red, white and blue.

When you braid any flat cord, be careful to keep each strand flat for the best results.

When sewing cord to a skirt or jacket in a pattern, draw the pattern on the wrong side and, using a fine needle with thread matching the cord, place the cord on the right side and follow the pattern lines from the back, catching the cord to the material with small stitches. If you are machine stitching the cord in place, you will need to mark the pattern on the right side.

Applique is another form of trim. Almost anything can be used for applique — cut-out cloth flowers, lace motifs or embroidered motifs. Some applique can be applied with a zig-zag stitch and some look better when done by hand. You can zig around a small printed flower or animal before cutting it from the material and you will have a finished edge on your applique.

Beautiful trims, by the yard, made of ribbon and silk threads to resemble a floral pattern, are available in some fabric shops but I find my best source for them at doll shows and ads in doll magazines.

Woven bands in beautiful colors and patterns make a nice trim, especially in rows on skirts.

Let us not forget the versatile rickrack braid. Its many sizes and colors lend themselves to all kinds of trims. You can use it showing only the points, all the points or none of the points, in rows of different sizes, in combinations of colors, or you can use two colors braided to form a trim. It can be applied with an embroidered stitch or made into rosettes. One of my husband's long, baby petticoats has a wide crocheted edge using a rickrack for a base for the pattern.

The popular feather stitch looks antique on garments, especially on underclothes.
The lazy daisy stitch can be caught in three places in each petal.

Some of the loveliest trim on baby doll garments is embroidery. There are many flosses and yarns that can be used with numerous embroidery stitches to enhance other garments as well. The feather stitch looks lovely on antique undergarments.

Beading is very elegant and is best on evening or bridal wear, and is a definite must for Indian costumes.

Long before the Indians had beads, they were decorating their clothes using porcupine quills, seeds and other natural things,

making handsome designs that expressed their love of beauty. Tribes could be recognized by their beadwork.

There are special long, slender, beading needles that work well for some bead work, but I also use a short, fine needle when stitching beads to a dainty gown.

I use fine seed pearls on the lace part of doll wedding gowns. Often, they are the cut-apart, rope type, so I glue them in place with a tiny bit of craft glue. If the glue is too thick, I thin it with a small amount of water. These

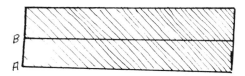

Bias material, when folded and stitched into a curved puff, can be rolled into roses and buds that make a nice trim.

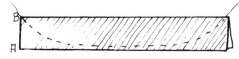

pearls look nice in clusters of two or three.

A nice bead trim on an all lace blouse is accomplished by a short double loop of beads, sewn at intervals all over the blouse and sleeves.

Some garments **need** buttons, not only to hold them together, but also for decorating. Many garments **look** better for using buttons. They can be the only trim on a garment. Often buttons, sewn on in groups, will look better than an even row.

Modern machines have many decorative stitches that often will be enough trim for a garment. Several even rows of straight stitches can trim a garment.

Ribbon and material flowers can add just the touch needed to change a garment from humdrum to a beauty. Cloth roses can be made by gathering narrow stripes of folded bias and

Back view.

The passion flower — button trim.

sewing the gathers together along the raw edges and a simple folding of ribbon can become buds or full blown roses.

Method: Tie a knot in the ribbon. Hold the ribbon in your right hand between the thumb and forefinger, pinching close to the knot. Bring the front piece of ribbon back behind the knot on the square.

Now, fold the second piece on the square. Continue to fold back, alternating the ribbon for at least 12 folds. After making one rose, you must decide how many folds you will want. When you have folded the ribbon a sufficient number of times, place the folded rose in the left hand between the thumb and forefinger and, while holding it, carefully pull one ribbon from the bottom, and a rose is formed.

Stitch at the bottom of the rose to prevent it from coming apart and cut off any excess ribbon. It can be set on a wire stem and the wire wrapped if you want to use the rose in a bouquet. Dainty little rolled roses made in silk ribbon are enchanting as trim for tiny dolls' clothing.

Last but not least, we look at feathers. Color is no problem because there are many. The lovely ostrich feathers can be used whole or split into small groups. They also curl beautifully by gently pulling them over a semi-sharp surface such as the edge of an unserrated table knife, while holding the feathers tightly with your thumb on the edge of the knife. Please pull gently to avoid breaking feathers. They can be wet and rolled on permanent wave rods and ruffled after drying. They can be carefully curled with a warm curling iron.

Braid trim.

Embroidered braid trim.

Trims that can be used in a continuous row or cut apart as motifs.

Chapter 9

Footwear — Booties to Boots

One can now buy practically any type of doll shoe needed for the many dolls in the world to-day and most are very lovely.

However this is a book on custom making dolls' clothing so we will start with a baby doll's foot-ware — the ever popular bootie. Generally any baby bootie pattern will fit a doll if it is made from very fine yarn, using a small hook; and elsewhere in this book I tell you how to get this yarn. I have used regular baby yarn for the 11″ Bye-Lo baby's crocheted booties, however.

The Bye-Lo doll bootie.

Here are directions for baby doll booties, using regular three-ply baby yarn and a size six, seven or eight crochet hook. Crochet a chain of 16 stitches.

Row 1. Two double crochet in fourth chain from hook. One dc in each of the next 10 chains, five dc in next chain, this makes the turn at the toe. One dc in each of the next 10 chains; two dc in the same chain as the first two dc. These two dc, the first two dc and the chain three make the turn for the heel of the bootie. Join at the top of chain three.

Row 2. Chain three, two dc in the next dc of first row. One dc in next 11 dc. Two dc in next four dc, this turns at the toe. One dc in the next 11 dc. Two dc in the next two dc, and one dc in the same dc as the chain three. Join at top of chain three.

Row 3. Chain three and one dc in each of the 37 dc of row two. Join at top of chain three.

Row 4. Chain three and dc in the next eight dc of row three. Decrease in next two dc as follows: Throw thread over hook as for a dc, put hook through dc on row three and pull yarn through (three yarns on hook); throw thread over hook as for another dc, four yarns on hook; put hook through next dc on row three and pull thread through five yarns on hook. Throw yarn over hook and pull through two yarns. One dc in next dc; decrease in next two dc, one dc in next dc; decrease the next two dc; one dc in next dc, decrease in next two dc; dc in next dc, decrease in next two dc. Dc in next dc, and a final decrease in the next two dc. One dc in next nine dc and join at top of chain three.

Row 5. Chain three, one dc in next nine dc, six decreases in next twelve dc, one dc in next 10 dc. Join at top of chain three.

Row 6. Chain one and one single crochet in each of the 26 dc. Join at chain one.

Row 7. Chain three. One dc in each of the 26 single crochet. Join at the top of chain three.

Row 8. Chain one and repeat Row 6.

Row 9. Chain three. One dc in single crochet in the same stitch as chain three. Make a picot by chain three and a slip stitch in the top of the last single crochet. A slip stitch is like a single crochet except you do not throw the thread over the hook, you just put the hook in the top of the dc and catch the yarn and pull it all the way through. Then continue with the next dc in the same single crochet as the chain three and dc with picot. You now have a shell with picot by making two dc in the same single crochet, a picot on top of second dc, one more dc in same shell. Continue until you have a three dc shell with picot in **every other** single crochet of the previous row; join at top of chain three. Cut the yarn about 3″ long and either thread a large eye needle and sew the yarn end in or work it in with the hook.

Lace ribbon through the double crochet row, between the two single crochet rows, to complete the bootie. Make the other bootie the same way with the same hook to get the same size.

To thread a needle with yarn, fold the end of a piece of yarn into a loop, hold the yarn near the loop between your left thumb

The same bootie with a different border and two rows of single crochet around the foot for trim.

and index finger. Place the flat end of the needle eye in the loop, and slide the loop and needle down further between your fingers until you cannot see the yarn. Pinch the yarn together very tight as you pull the yarn upward with the needle, but do not pull the yarn up far enough that you can see more than just a tiny bit. As you are pulling the yarn up, also gradually slide the needle out while continuing to pinch the yarn.

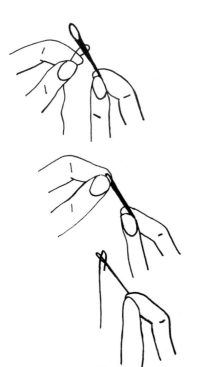

To thread a needle with yarn first fold the end of the yarn into a loop and slip the eye end of the needle between the loop. Now slide your two fingers up until they cover the yarn. Pinch the yarn tightly between your fingers while pulling up and out with needle until the needle is out. Continue pinching the yarn and slip the eye of the needle down between your fingers over the yarn.

Now slide the needle eye down over the speck of yarn showing and slip the needle over the yarn as you carefully release it. Another way is to cut a piece of paper into a narrow strip about 1" long and fold it over double with the yarn at the fold. Let the short end of the yarn hang out about an inch; clip the end of the paper to a point from one corner down in a slanting cut and, using

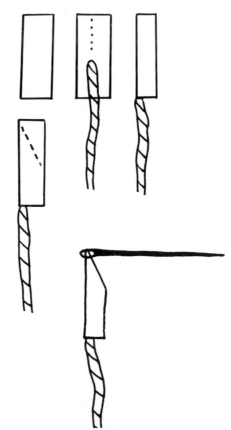

Another way to thread yarn on a needle is to place the end of the yarn in the center of a short length of paper and fold the paper in half enclosing the yarn, cut the paper to a point and thread the paper and yarn through the needle's eye.

the folded paper as a guide, thread the needle.

With all the doll shoes on the market there is one doll that seems to be unable to wear a commercial shoe. He has an adorable foot, but the charm of a big toe that turns up is lost when trying to fit him with shoes because it sticks out in such a way that it's impossible to get a regular shoe on his foot and have it look nice. Usually feet of this nature are on baby dolls, and a bootie or soft shoe made of cloth can solve the problem. But the doll I am referring to looks so nice dressed in a little boy's velvet suit that booties look out of place. I solved the problem by putting him in sandals.

Even with a sandal, there was a problem because the big toe curled forward far enough that the sole poked out and looked awkward. To solve that problem I slipped a needle, threaded with double thread, through the stitching around the sole and

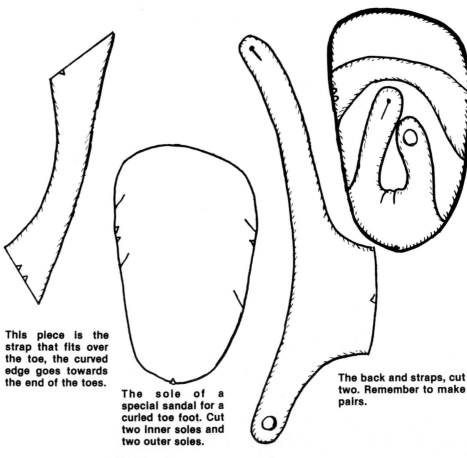

This piece is the strap that fits over the toe, the curved edge goes towards the end of the toes.

The sole of a special sandal for a curled toe foot. Cut two inner soles and two outer soles.

The back and straps, cut two. Remember to make pairs.

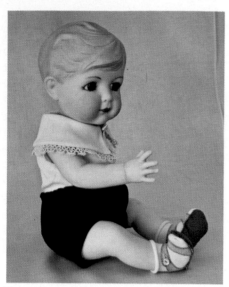
The pattern of the sandal made up.

Cloth shoes.

pulled it, as one would a drawstring, until the sole fell into a natural curve toward the toe, and then it looked fine.

The pattern for this sandal is in this chapter and the instructions for making are as follows:

Cut the back strap, front sandal piece and inner sole from Ultra Suede, suede cloth or whatever you are using for the shoes. It's best not to use any leather heavier than the Cabretta cut because the sandals need to be soft. If you are using a material, it's best to also use a lining. They should either be fused together or glued together.

Follow the directions on the fusing paper for that method. When I glue material together before cutting, I spread a thin layer of glue on each piece to be joined and then place them together, pulling and stretching to make sure they are joined. I then lay the piece flat and push out in all directions from the center, turn the piece over and repeat the process.

Often I lay the piece on paper towelling and thumbtack it to a board. I cover it with more paper towels and apply weight. After it's dry, I cut out the shoes.

Now back to the sandal — you have the upper parts and inner

soles cut according to the directions on the pattern. You now need a bottom sole. This is cut the same size as the inner sole, and can be of the same material as the uppers but it does look nice if it's a little darker, even if of the same material. The sandals shown are made of Ultra Suede in two colors.

Either hand overcast or zig overcast around the indicated sections on the upper parts only. Stitch the inner sole and the bottom sole together — remember to make them in a pair as this sandal does have a left and a right. Place the upper parts at the indicated place on the soles and hand overcast or zig stitch around the sole, catching the upper sections to the sole.

Make a buttonhole in the longer strap and try on the doll's foot for button placement. If the sandal sole doesn't curve to the toe, correct the trouble with the method already given.

One doesn't always have to make a shoe because some dolls come with molded shoes that are painted. However, you may want to embellish them. For example: I enjoy making and dressing a modern lady with molded high heels, and often her costume would not be complete unless she had fancy shoes. As I dress most of these dolls in bridal attire, I given them lace shoes. This can be done by gluing lace cutouts in a pattern on the molded shoe and using a bit of leather for the soles. Sometimes a ribbon rosette will be all the shoe needs.

A piece of self fabric can be glued to the shoe and a cord of embroidery thread in the same color glued around the edge with a small bow or buckle to complete the shoe.

Some dolls can wear baby or children's shoes but sometimes these shoes need to be altered for a better fit. I have found that lowering the back section and

resetting the strap and buckle can make a big difference.

Because of the variety of doll shoes available and the number of doll shoe patterns on the market, customizing a shoe isn't difficult.

Sometimes a bit of embroidery, lace or other trim will decorate a ready-made shoe to match a costume. And if the doll shoe pattern doesn't fit your doll, cut one in paper towelling and adjust it until you have what you want.

Shoes can be made of most any material. Some suggestions follow: fabric lined or even inner lined with a cotton fleece for thickness; velveteen with leather; two colors of leather, lace over fabric, Ultra Suede, suede cloth, velvet, fur or fur cloth.

Leather comes in several thicknesses depending on the cut. The Cabretta cut is one of the best for the upper part of the shoe, using a thicker cut for the soles, including an extra piece for a heel if one is needed.

Inner soles can be cardboard.

A good way to be sure you are making a right and a left shoe is to mark the cardboard insole with an R on one and an L on the other. Mark both sides of the insole. It also helps to mark each piece of the shoe.

All styles can be made, but I do not have a formula in measuring to give you because the method I use is to cut it in paper towelling and fit until I have what I want.

I make the boots with two pieces for the tops, seamed up the back so they fit nicely at the ankle area and seamed up the middle front over the toes, leaving an opening to be laced. Then they are sewn or glued to the sole. It's simple but looks fine for some outfits and works very well for Eskimo Muk Luks.

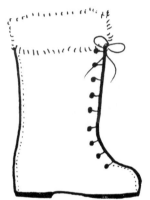

The upper part of these boots are two pieces stitched at the back and over the toe.

This soft slipper is attractive with a ruffle of lace or ribbon for trim.

A heel and toe of a contrasting material or color decorates one shoe while stitching and buttons is enough for another and embroidery trims yet another.

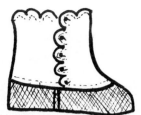

These spats can become leggings by making them longer.

I use a regular leather glue when gluing the shoe to the soles. It holds better than craft glue.

Generally the shoes fit the soles just fine when clipped around the bottom edge but if the doll has a high instep or fat foot, sometimes more top is needed and I find that if I stitch a gathering row around the shoe bottom before clipping, it will help hold any excess shoe in and fit the sole very well.

Some ideas for trims on shoes are given in other chapters. In addition, consider making them in two colors or in white with colored laces or buttons, or buy white leather and dye it the color needed. Try a silk bias binding and a lace ruffle at the top or embroidered motifs down the side or on the toe. Lace with ribbon flowers is also pretty.

A felt hat to match felt shoes is another idea. Try your ideas — the result may surprise and please you.

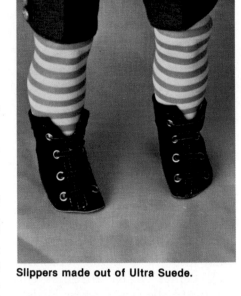

Slippers made out of Ultra Suede.

Little leather shoes.

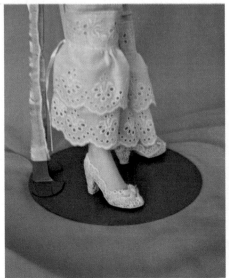

Lace shoes.

Navy blue leather shoes made from the pockets of a lady's leather coat.

Chapter 10
Baby Doll Clothing and Wrappings

What is more appealing and sweet than the wee babe in a long christening gown? A popular baby doll that seems to be a must is the ever-charming Bye-Lo baby.

We gave a few ideas for enhancing her body in Chapter 1. Now we will dress her. Remember, start from the bottom out.

To make a diaper, measure her waist and the distance from the back center waist through the legs up to the front center waist.

A baby doll dress.

A Bye-Lo baby dress.

Another Bye-Lo baby doll dress.

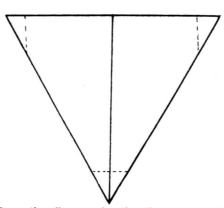

Draw the diagram for the diaper and cut where indicated.

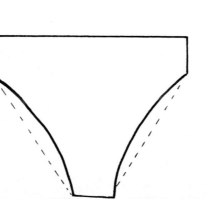

Trim off the excess material for a nice fit.

Now, draw a line representing the waist. Make it as long as the waist measurement. From the center, draw a line straight down as long as the measurement through the crotch. Join the ends and you have a triangle.

But we don't want a simple triangle diaper, so cut some from each point, more from the down point than the others. Make a curve on each side so the diaper will not be so bunchy between the legs.

Cut a pattern from a paper towel and try it on the baby doll. Fold the side first. Bring the bottom piece through the legs, place over the side pieces and pin. Is it too high in back? If so, trim it down a little. Do the legs gap, okay, take a tuck. Make any other adjustments needed.

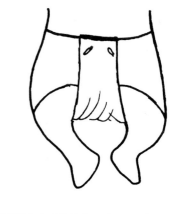

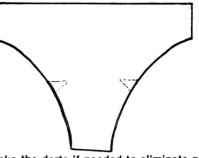

Make the darts if needed to eliminate gaping.

Now cut the diaper from the material you are using and fold in any tucks. Zig a narrow lace all around the diaper and pin it on the baby doll.

You may notice that the doll pictured isn't what one would call a true Bye-Lo. I like the Bye-Lo baby doll the way Grace Putnam created her but I also like to do them "my way," with wide open eyes and often a cute wig and elegant clothing.

I've suggested making all the underthings first but this dress and slip will be the exception to the rule. As we proceed, you will see how easy it is to make the slip pattern from the dress pattern. You could make the dress pattern from the slip pattern but this way is best.

Let's try and make her pattern without marking her body because, as you become more proficient in pattern making, you will be able to make them without marking the dolls.

The dress has a yoke so measure from the shoulder straight down to the spot you want the yoke to end. Here we will make a pin marking. Make this mark at the arm and the body seam line. A good yoke length is about ¾" up from where the bottom of the arm comes out of the doll's body. Mark the place with a pin; measure the other side the same length and mark with a pin. Lay the tape measure from pin to pin and mark the line with more pins. This is the only marking needed.

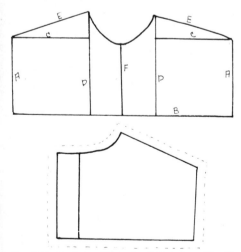

Draft the yoke pattern, both front and back.

On a piece of paper draw a straight line down the length of the measurement. Measure across the chest to the same spot on the opposite side and draw a line to match on the paper. Mea-

sure the shoulder and draw a line to match on the paper. Measure the shoulder and draw a line that length across from the top of the first line. Measure from the neck at the shoulder down to the bottom of the yoke. Draw that line on the paper. Now draw a new shoulder line creating the shoulder slant. Measure from the center front to the yoke line and draw the corresponding line on the paper. Now, draw a neckline and the yoke pattern is ready to make. Remember to allow the seams. Do the back the same way and allow for a back opening.

To make the skirt pattern, use the original yoke not the seam-allowed pattern. Measure down, at the yoke side end, the distance of the arm and mark it on the paper.

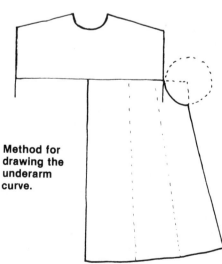

The skirt pattern.

Method for drawing the underarm curve.

Start at the yoke bottom side corner and draw a ¼ circle the length of the arm from yoke to underarm. It may be easier to draw a circle and cut it into

fourths. This is the underarm curve and the top of the skirt. Draw a slanting line down the side and a straight line down from the center front. The length will depend on the length you want the skirt to be. I usually put a 6" ruffle on my Bye-Lo baby dresses, and that measurement is considered when planning the dress length.

Make the skirt the same length all across the skirt as the length of the center line. There will be a slight curving toward the side of the skirt because of the A-line cut. You will want fullness in the skirt; add enough so the top of the skirt will be twice the size of bottom of the yoke. Make the skirt pattern, allowing seams, and no material for tucks will be needed as we will make simulated tucks described in Chapter 8.

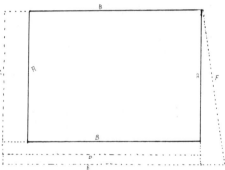

The sleeve pattern for the upreaching arms.

Because the arms are reaching up, the top of the sleeve will not need to be higher than the underarm. So measure the underarm for length and draw a line that length. Measure around the armseye and draw lines that length on the square across from the top and bottom of the first line, keeping them an equal distance apart. This is the actual sleeve size, we want a little fullness around so add 1" to the length of the sleeve. A ruffle will also look nice at the wrist so add the amount you want for a ruffle—Wait! If you sew lace on the ruffle, you will not need as much material for the ruffle. Take that

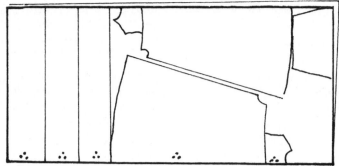

The material layout; the material left over can be used for the bonnet.

into consideration when adding for the ruffle.

Now one more thing. The sleeves do look nice with a little more fullness at the wrist. Add it by drawing a line down from the underarm to the wrist on a slant to add extra fullness. Now, make the pattern and we are ready to cut the dress.

I find that three lengths of 42-44" material makes a nice full ruffle. Pull a thread and cut the ruffles from one selvage across to the other selvage before cutting the dress. By pulling a thread, your ruffles will be even and the fabric will have a straight edge.

To determine the amount of material required for the dress, lay the pattern out on a piece of paper folded to half the width of the material you plan to buy. If the material is 45", lay the pattern on a 22" piece following the diagram shown above.

The slip is cut exactly the same, except there will not be any sleeves.

The original Bye-Lo wore a sheer cotton christening dress with a lace-trimmed cotton slip. I like to dress my babies a little fancier so I use a sheer, soft organdy-type material for the dress and bonnet; a lining material and sheer tricot for the over slip.

The two slip materials are sewn as one through the bodice but the skirts hang separately. The slip skirts each have a lace-trimmed ruffle the same width as the dress ruffle. Place the tricot bodice pieces on the lining pieces and sew the shoulder seams. Place the tricot skirt pieces on the lining pieces and sew two gathering rows across the tops. Pull the thread and sew to the bodice with the gathers even.

Zig a row of lace around the neck and armholes by placing the outside edge of the lace even with the edge of the neckline and ziging along the inside or straight edge. Now trim away the excess material from behind the lace close to the zig stitching. Zig overcast the back opening edge down to the waist and zig lace to one side of the pieced ruffles, both the lining and the tricot.

Sew both skirts together at the side seams from the underarm down 3". Sew the side seams separately the rest of the way down the side seams. Gather and sew the ruffles to the bottom of the skirts, then sew a row of lace over the seam.

I usually top stitch the seam with a zig stitch and then trim away the excess material before stitching a row of lace to hide the stitch line. The two skirts are now sewn up the back separately leaving an opening for placing the slip on the doll.

Close the back with snaps. I usually use the metal size 04 snaps but recently I have found a clear plastic snap that is practically invisible that I like very much.

Now for her dress. Set your machine for a narrow zig stitch and try it on a scrap of the dress material. You will want the stitch to look nice without puckering or pulling. I find that when I zig stitch tucks, that it helps to gently control the material both before and behind the needle by holding the fabric gently.

After getting the setting to your satisfaction, make a note of the setting because we will need it again; but for now, zig tuck six lines down the center of the yoke of the dress about ¼" apart. You could use the pressure foot as a guide to get them even. Next, using a straight stitch, sew the shoulder seams and piece the ruffle leaving an open end.

Zig lace along the edge of the ruffle, the bottom of the sleeves and around the neck.

Now lay the bodice flat and arrange insertion lace over the shoulders to a point in the center front. Stitch the lace to the bodice on the inside edge only at this time. Gather and sew the skirt pieces to the bodice and sew a row of lace through the sleeves, for decoration, up far enough so it will not be too close to the elastic at the wrist. Sew the insertion lace on both edges.

Now measure the elastic and make a zig casing over it at the wrist. See Chapter 2 for zig casing method. Sew a row of ribbon over the waist seam in the front and back.

Sew in the sleeves without catching the lace at the shoulder. Gather some lace and place it under the outer edge of the insertion lace on the bodice and stitch the laces to the bodice together. If you wish, ribbon can be placed under the insertion lace for trim before sewing it to the dress.

Sew the side seams and sew the gathered ruffles to the bottom of the skirt. Zig top stitch the ruffle skirt seam and sew a row of gathered lace along the seam. Trim the excess material from the back of the seam. Sew several rows of insertion lace on the skirt with one row meeting the gathered lace at the seam. Now back to the zig tuck setting, and trim the skirt and ruffles with row after row of simulated tucks.

You can sew the back of the dress before doing the tucking if you wish.

Directions for the bonnet will be found in Chapter 6.

For a tiny baby doll, make the christening outfit from a beautiful embroidered linen handkerchief. Look for one that has a nice border all around and a small embroidered pattern in each corner because more elaborate embroidery will overwhelm the doll.

Another baby doll dress.

A baby dress from the early 1900s that has beautiful hand-embroidered insertion and eyelet ruffles.

A baby dress worn in 1906.

As the doll is so small, avoid bulkiness by having a simple A-line slip with lace trim. These tiny garments always look best when they are hand sewn. Use a fine needle and thread, take the smallest stitches possible and you will have excellent results. Remember not to use knots and to backtrack your endings.

Make the outfit look like a dress and a coat by having a solid dress front under a split front. Use the edges and squares of two of the handkerchief corners; one edge of each for the

Baby doll dress with ribbons and rosettes.

A doll dressed in a 1906 homemade baby dress that was used for a christening dress.

bottom and the other edge up the center front.

each for the bottom and the other edge up the center front.

If you have some antique or favorite baby clothes that you wish to display, let a large doll wear them. Perhaps they need to be carefully taken in to fit the doll. To do this without cutting the garment, use any of the following suggestions that will work for your garment.

If the shoulders are too wide, make a tuck large enough for the correct fit that, when folded over, will be covered by the sleeve (shoulder seam). If the sleeves are too long, you can also make a tuck around the sleeve at the armseye, inside the dress. The shoulder tuck will cover any evidence of the sleeve tuck.

If the neck is too low, take a dart in the neck at the shoulder line. Sometimes a box pleat in the front of the dress at the neckline will look alright. A too large neck can also be made to fit by hand stitching around the edge and gathering it, or hand stitching down the neck edge about ¼" and forming a soft ruffle when the stitches are pulled.

The baby clothing from the 1930's was pretty but of a simple cut, usually without shoulder seams or set-in sleeves.

Most of the given methods will work with these clothes with the addition of sewing the sleeves from the inside on a slant to a small opening, this avoids that huge sleeve look.

Usually these old garments are so soft from the many washings they have received that I use a spray starch to give them some body. I always press the embroidery from the wrong side and carefully mend any broken places in the crochet or embroidery.

A crocheted set.

Baby dolls look nice in crocheted jackets, booties and bonnets, and there are many patterns on the market for these sets to be made in real baby size. These patterns can be adapted to baby dolls by using a small crochet hook and fine yarn. It's very difficult to find yarn fine enough, but some two or three-ply yarns can be split and will work very well.

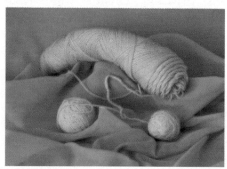
Dividing the yarn.

It takes time and patience to split the yarn but I've found a way that is easy. If the yarn pulls from the center, pull out a length

and start winding one strand on a spool and the other strand on another spool. Every so often, hold onto both spools, which have had the strands wound on evenly, and let the yarn hang. It will spin around and unwind so you can put more on the spools. Repeat until all yarn has been transferred to the spools into balls. If the yarn pulls out of the center of the skein too fast, pin it with a safety pin.

If you are separating three-ply baby yarn the method to use is different. Separate the yarn onto two spools with the one-ply on one spool and the two-ply on the other by pulling the one-ply so the two-ply slides along the one-ply as far as possible. If the one-ply hasn't already broken, break it and wind it on a spool.

This extra fine yarn is great for the teeny-tiny baby doll things. As you crochet or knit with these broken pieces, simply lay one end over the other for an inch or so and continue crocheting, knots are not necessary.

Silk sewing thread can be added to the single-ply and the two crocheted as one for a lovely silky look. These small crocheted things are lovely.

In Chapter 9 is a recipe for crocheting booties for an 11" Bye-Lo baby doll. They are made using a double crochet stitch. For smaller babies, use the same pattern with a single crochet stitch.

Baby yarns make beautiful afghans for dolls but again I find that the fine yarn is better for the smaller ones. The ones pictured are made from one-ply of a three-ply yarn from France which is no longer manufactured.

These tiny afghans are made in a variety of stitches but the one that I like best is very simple. There is a center section of the crochet pattern, then a beading section and last, a border. I will give the basic instructions,

presuming that you already know how to crochet.

SMALL DOLL AFGHAN

Make a chain the desired width of the center section.

Row 1: Chain one, single crochet in second chain from hook, double crochet in third chain from hook, single crochet in next chain and repeat DC and C in the chain stitches for the first row, ending with a DC.

Row 2: Chain one, single C in top of DC of first row, DC in the next single C of first row; repeat to the end of the row, ending with a DC. Repeat **Row 2** until you have the desired size of the center section of the afghan. I usually make it longer than the width so the afghan is not square when finished.

For the beading section, single crochet all around the afghan with three single C in each corner. End row by joining to the first single C of that row.

Row 3: Chain three and make a double crochet in single crochet of the former row. Put three or five DC in each corner, whichever amount makes the corner lay nice and flat, join to the top of chain three at beginning of row.

Row 4: Chain one and single crochet in each stitch. You can

Using a crocheted afghan as a wrap.

Using an afghan as a cover.

make any border you wish. The one pictured has a lover's knot border with a shell edge.

How to make a lover's knot stitch: Loosen the loop on the hook until it is ¼" long. Keep this size in mind because that is your gauge for the knot stitch for this size afghan. Okay, you have a ¼" loop, now bring the hook in front of the loop and put it through the loop and hook the yarn. Bring the yarn through the loop and hook the yarn again — you have three yarns on your hook. Catch the yarn again and pull it through all three.

Now, yarn over the hook and pull it through tight. This isn't usually done but I find it locks the knot in place and looks fine.

Loosen the loop to ¼" and bring the hook in front of the loop, through the loop and hook the yarn; again, through the loop and hook the yarn, so there are three yarns on the hook. Place the yarn over the hook and pull through all three. This time do not throw the thread over and pull tight, but put the hook in the first single crochet of the last row, hook the yarn and pull it through. Throw the yarn over the hook and pull tight. Pull the yarn on hook to a ¼" loop and make another knot stitch. When it is completed, put it in the next single crochet.

This may seem too full to you, but with three or four rows of knot stitches it will make a lovely full ruffle.

If you want the edge to be flatter, skip every other single crochet. When you get to the last knot, do only the first part of the stitch to the point where you pull the stitch tight. Now, instead of making a ¼" loop, make a double crochet down into the chain stitch. This will leave the hook at the top of the knot all ready to start the second row of knot stitches. I suggest you throw the yarn over the hook and pull it tight at this place also.

Now make a second row of knot stitches, catching each one in the knot of the previous row by putting the hook through two of the strands in the knot. End this row also with a DC. Put it in the knot where you started the second row. Repeat for a third row.

Edge: Chain three, make a DC in the same stitch as the beginning of chain; make a picot by chaining three and a single crochet in the beginning of the chain three. One more DC in the same place as the last DC. Now, make two DC in the top of the next knot through two strands of yarn. Make a picot and another DC. You have made two shells in two of the knot stitches for the edge. Continue to make shells until the edge is completed, ending with a slip stitch in the top of the chain three of the first shell. Weave the end of the yarn into the shells.

Thread ribbon through the beading and tie the ends into a

An eyelet-trimmed quilt.

nice bow.

Lovely doll quilts can be made of one or two colors of tricot, quilted in a design or tied with yarn. There are small, patterned quilt materials available in most fabric stores that look nice either quilted or tied. Be careful to not use too much batting in the small quilts, as they will be stiff and bulky.

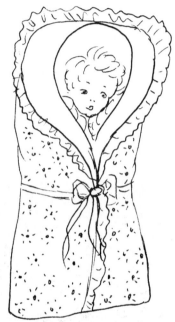
A slip-in cover for the baby doll. The tie can hold the doll in place.

For baby doll coverups or wrappings, the tiny baby doll will look adorable in a slip-in bunting. Use two pieces of soft fabric 8"x7". The 7" will be the length of the finished bunting so round off the two top corners on both pieces.

If you are using two colors, decide which color you want for the outside and place it right side up on a thin piece of padded cotton or batting cut the same size as the fabric. Pin it together and sew gathered lace or eyelet around the rounded top part, starting down at the corner, back to the other corner, none on the bottom. Sew this on the edge with lace or eyelet right-side down to the fabric's right side. Place this part on the other cut piece and stitch around the edge

Another cover for the baby doll that is quite fancy.

A coverup called the nightengale.

A cover-all suit made using the pant pattern along with the bodice pattern.

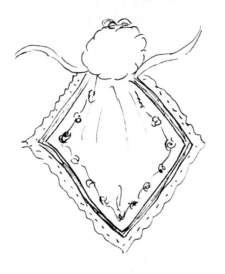

A wrap with a hood called a nightengale.

A fancy bunting.

enclosing the lace. Do not sew the bottom at this time. Clip the curves and a few places on the straight for good measure and turn the bunting.

If you wish, you can tie the bunting as you would a quilt, having the fine yarn on the outside side. This really isn't needed but it can be done. Pin all of the raw edges at the bottom together to keep them in place. Lay the bunting flat with the right side down, put a pin half-way across the bottom to mark the center back.

Fold the right side under with the edge (not the lace edge) a little past the center back. Fold the left side over to lap over the right side a little past the center back.

Stitch across the bottom of the bunting. Turn right side out and either catch the front together with a stitch or two, or sew on a snap. Sew a length of ribbon at the center back where it will fit around and help hold the doll in place when tied in a bow in front.

This type of bunting has numerous possibilities. You can make it for larger dolls, you can edge it with self material or ruffles, even bind it with ribbon. A hood with a collar could be made to match and look very nice.

There is a cute old-fashioned doll coverup called a "Nightengale." I don't know why — perhaps it was worn at night. To make one, take a square of cloth, round off one corner and sew a casing through which ribbon or elastic can be threaded to make a cap to fit the doll's head. Set the casing back in enough to make the edge ruffle when the ribbon is inserted. Sew on ties for holding on the cap and wrap the rest of the fabric around the doll. The entire outside edge can be finished as desired.

Another coverup is a hooded snow suit type. Using the information in the previous chapters, you can make one and even figure out how to put feet in it.

A row of eyelet or lace around the face is attractive and the hood can come to a point with a tassle or pom-pom at the point.

A suit for a boy doll could have teddy-bear ears and a pom-pom tail, or rabbit ears look nice on either a boy or girl baby doll.

Baby dress from the 1930's. Handmade slip with a crocheted edge.

Another 1930 baby dress.

Notice how pretty the green is on the baby.

A Bye-Lo baby doll dress in a crocheted outfit made of fine yarn and using a small hook and a real baby pattern.

A small dress made from a lady's handkerchief.

Japanese silk, 25 years old.

This dress front is trimmed with lace and appliqued squares of embroidery.

Flannel blankets can be made for baby dolls from yardage and bound in ribbon. Sometimes two colors or a print and a plain color look nice when sewn together and edged with eyelet or bound with ribbon.

Whatever you do will please a little girl as they love to wrap up their dolls.

Same pattern, different babies.

Chapter 11

Fabrics and Fur

Fur trim on a costume.

I think that most people who sew will have yardage tucked away to make something someday and, as you become involved with dressing dolls, not only are the pieces brought out, but also all the little bits and treasures that have been cached away through the years, are retrieved as well. Soon you are haunting every garage sale, doll show, flea market, thrift store and any other place where you hope to find a treasure in a bit of old lace, antique silk or other material that you think you simply must have for that doll. Well, join the crowd—I too have literally box after box of material that I'm going to use someday, and it has become necessary to mark the boxes so when a piece is needed I will know where to look.

This passion of dressing dolls in antique material made from natural fibers is fine if you are duplicating an antique doll, but let's be realistic. In this day and age, with modern technology, man can duplicate the natural fibers and produce very fine

materials. Remember that what we produce now will be tomorrow's antiques. That is why I put porcelain bodies on most of my dolls; because if any of them reach antiquity, I should like the body, as well as the head, to be preserved.

This pertains to clothing as well. Often antique silk, however lovely, has deteriorated until it hangs in shreds. Regardless of what I have just said, we are still going to use the old fabrics when we have them. So here are a few hints on caring for and restoring some of these materials.

One problem usually found in old garments is discoloring. They often turn yellow or brown. If the material is cotton, the white color can be fairly well restored using the following formula. Use one tablespoon of Basic H, a Shaklee product, to one gallon of clear water and soak the garment or material for a few days, turning it every once in a while, until the whiteness has been restored. Lace can be brightened in this solution also.

To dry lace so no pressing is required, arrange it while it is still wet on a flat surface, gently putting each loop in place. If the lace is badly torn, place it on a piece of net with holes approximately the same size as the lace net holes, and catch the lace and net together.

The nap on velvets can usually be revived by steaming and sometimes, depending on the velvet, you can restore it by placing it in the clothes dryer with a damp wash cloth.

Often a sheer material that needs an undergarment for a lining will look better if you sew the two materials as one. Any tucks can be sewn in the sheer only, and then the lining cut to fit.

Some of the fabrics I use for baby dolls and child dolls are found in almost all of the fabric stores. I use batiste, percale, dotted swiss, eyelet, small prints, soft materials, silk organza, nylon organdy, cotton organdy, novelty weaves, white on white, linen, gingham, narrow wale corduroy, velours, velveteen, silk prints, taffeta and satin.

The French dolls are dressed more elaborately using rich trims and laces. The materials I find more appropriate for them are taffetas, brocades, satin, velvets, metallics, gabardine, fine woolens, chiffon, crepe-de-chine, georgettes, crepe and silks.

The German dolls also wore fine fabrics with less elaborate trimming and the modern dolls look fine in many materials.

It isn't just the material that is important but what you do with it as well. So plan carefully and reap the harvest of satisfaction with a beautiful garment from beautiful fabric.

Working with fur can be a challenge but if you follow these rules you will be delighted with the results.

First, decide what you are going to use the fur for. Let's make a collar and muff set. Cut **two** collar patterns exactly the size needed but do not allow any seams. It's not necessary to allow seams on fur. Cut one collar pat-

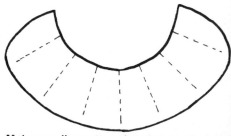

Make a collar pattern but do not allow the seams. Mark the pattern but before slitting the pattern, make a duplicate.

Split the pattern and cut it in two at the center back.

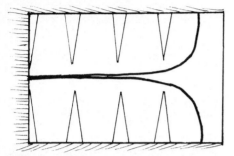

Mark the pattern on the fur as shown.

tern so it is flat, by cutting from the neckline to the collar edge.

Now cut another paper pattern with the collar spread. Mark the cuts. These cuts are now gores. Fold the pattern in two at the center back. Lay this half pattern on the skin side of the fur with the fur laying to the back and the center back of the collar toward the fur that lays back.

Mark with tailor's chalk on dark skin, and a pencil on light skin, around the pattern, marking all of the gores. Now turn the pattern over and mark the other half of the collar.

Using a sharp razor blade or a feather scalpel, carefully cut the skin only, not the hairs. This works best if you raise the skin up from the surface.

Thread a small fine needle with matching single thread. Some people use a leather needle but I haven't found one fine enough and the other needle works well for me.

Place the two collar pieces together at the back center seam with the fur sides together. You can hold it so the skins touch and no hairs are coming through. Now whip stitch overcast the seam together with the stitches

close. Do the same with all of the gores and the collar should now be pretty close to being the same as the first pattern. Now you can see why I had you cut two.

Using the remaining collar pattern, cut a collar from outing flannel or thin bonded batting, without allowing any seams. Next, allowing seams, cut a collar lining using the garment lining or a matching material. Set these two collars aside.

Use some seam tape, twill tape or lining selvage about ½" wide and place the woven edge along the edge of the collar on the fur side. Whip stitch the tape and fur edge together all around the collar.

When rounding the collar curve in front, pull slightly on the tape as you sew, to make the round corner curve under. When sewing the tape around the inside curve of the collar neckline, allow a small pleat in the tape in three or four places to allow for the tape to lay flat when it is folded back.

Place the flannel or batting collar on the skin side of the col-

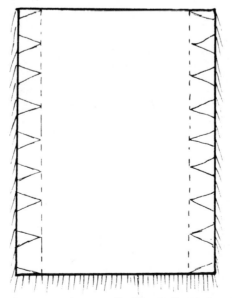

The pattern for a muff with small openings for the hands.

lar and fold the tape over the edge and stitch to the flannel.

Baste a hem all around the lining collar piece and pin it in place over the flannel collar. Hand sew the two together, making sure the lining covers the edge. Notice how nice the center back of the collar looks with the nap of the fur coming together. The collar is now ready to hand stitch to the garment.

To make the muff, decide whether you want a flat or round muff. We will do the round one, and I'm sure you can do the flat one by following the same principle without using gores. The muff is cut with the fur running down. To make the pattern, pin five darts in each side of a rectangular piece of paper or paper towelling, leaving an opening larger than needed for the hands. Keep the darts short and even.

Now cut the darts out and lay the pattern on the skin side of the fur. Mark and cut. Sew the fur together as instructed for the collar. Sew all the darts. Sew tape around each hand hole. Cut a lining and make a tube to fit the hand holes but not as long as the muff. Pleat or gather a matching ribbon ruffle, or make them from the lining material, for each hand hole. Turn the muff right side out and put several layers of padding around the muff inside.

Pin through the fur with corsage pins to hold the padding in place. Sew the ruffles either to the openings in the fur or in the lining, and hand stitch the lining in place with the ruffle showing. A lining or cord strap can also be attached to aid in holding the muff. Or, a cord can be attached at each side of the muff so that it can be hung around the neck. When making other fur pieces, use the same method.

Chapter 12
Dressing a Doll from a Picture

It has been my pleasure for over 25 years to dress beautiful happy brides, and to help make their wedding day a joyful event when they were attired in the gown of their dreams. Often these gowns were copies of dresses pictured in various bridal magazines.

A modern wedding gown from a 1982 magazine.

A close-up of the veil.

I've continued this practice of dressing brides...however, they are lady dolls. (I think a wedding

A bride doll dress after the fashion in the magazine. I call her my modern day "Pinkie."

My interpretation of the back.

doll look like she is playing dress-up and is not appropriate.)

In 1982 I found a picture of a beautiful wedding gown in a magazine and simply had to transform it to a doll. So I created it for an 18" lady doll and called her my modern day "Pinkie."

What is "Pinkie" without a "Blue Boy." So I dressed a male doll in a blue tuxedo and called him my modern day "Blue Boy."

A picture from a magazine.

My modern day "Blue Boy."

The bridal gown is as close to the one in the picture as I could make it with the materials and lace available. I did, however, take liberties by adding a longer train with elaborate lace detail. Also I gave her a long pink satin sash that fell from the back of the cumberbund. I had planned to make small silk roses but other flowers looked so lovely in her hair that I used them.

The English net used for the gown was the nearest I could find to the dotted material in the picture. The dots in the net were small and seemed in proportion to the doll's size.

Proportion is important to remember when copying a picture. The lace in the picture appeared to be Shiffli embroidered roses and leaves. I substituted a venetian-type heavy lace that had a similar look.

Often when doing a dress for a doll from a pictured adult, the exact materials in miniature just aren't available so do the best you can with what you can find. I think she makes a charming bride!

Another favorite bride doll is dressed from a sketch of an 1840 wedding dress imported from France and worn by a Southern belle. The original sketch is in a costume book found in most libraries called "The Mode in Costume." I dressed her to resemble Scarlett O'Hara in her mother's wedding dress, becoming the bride of Charlie Hamilton in the book "Gone With the Wind."

The original pictured gown was fashioned in embroidered satin and pleated chiffon and I was very fortunate to find a love-

A line drawing of a beautiful 1840 wedding gown from Paris used as a model for a gown on a doll representing Scarlett O'Hara.

ly, white embroidered satin ruffle material; but I had a problem with the pleated chiffon because it was edged with heavy red thread. The solution to that problem was simple. I cut away

the red edge and zig overcast a new edge in white. I could have left the cut edge unstitched but, as the pleating was on the bias, I

An old-fashioned doll in her undies.

A back view of her corset showing how it helps support the doll stand.

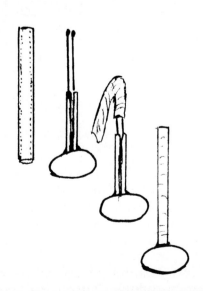

The stand support covered with satin ribbon.

felt that in time it would have a fuzzed look, and the zig stitch not only finished the edge nicely but gave it a fluted look as well.

As I mentioned before, make and dress the doll in her underclothing before doing the dress, which is exactly what I did to Scarlett. Her first bit of underwear was an eyelet camisole with ribbon-laced straps. Her pantaloons are white cotton with two ruffles of eyelet on each leg and a waistband that buttons.

Next she put on her corset which was laced in back and served a dual purpose. It not only served as part of her clothing, it also helped hold the doll stand in place. Her doll stand was made to slip up under her shoulder plate, camisole and corset. Because I wanted her to be special, I even made a tube from satin ribbon and slipped it down over the stand post so nothing would detract from her loveliness.

A view of her wedding gown.

Her bouffant crinoline was put on. I made the hoops by stitching several layers of horsehair braid in rows on the inside of the crinoline. The crinoline has a drawstring at the waist.

Her last bit of underclothing was a white, cotton petticoat with an eyelet ruffle. Her shoes

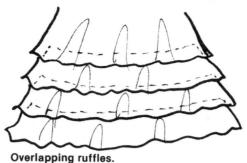
Overlapping ruffles.

are lace with a satin bow.

Now for the gown — when looking at a picture that you wish to copy, first analyze the construction and decide whether it was made all in one piece or more. When I looked at the sketch I felt that I'd have my best success if I made the dress in three sections and then combined them into one; so, first came the lovely ruffled skirt. I measured the skirt length and counted the number of ruffles pictured. I could see that the top ruffle really belonged to the bodice section rather than the skirt so I allowed for it but didn't sew it to the skirt lining.

Remember that ruffles need to set up inside each other to give the proper look. There are some exceptions for certain ruffle treatments, but as a general rule, set them overlapping.

You will notice that the ruffles alternate with a pleated row on the bottom in the picture. However, when I placed the ruffles on the lining, I found that I needed an extra ruffle to accommodate the overlapping and still achieve the proper length. So my copy of the picture has an extra ruffle, but I don't feel that it detracts.

I needed the extra ruffle because my ruffles were about ¼-½" too narrow. This was due to being unable to get an embroidered ruffle any wider than what I found, and cutting off the red edge on the pleated chiffon shortened that ruffle because a zig hem on bias uses about ¼" of material.

I left a 3-4" opening down the back of the skirt, which was held together with pins after placing it on the doll.

I next made the bodice of the gown, leaving the yoke for the last. I felt the construction would be easier if I made a full bodice from neck to shoulder to the bottom of the waistline and set the sleeves in. The yoke could then be made last and fitted over the bodice.

Both the bodice and yoke had to be lined, and I sewed the satin and lining together as one material. Again I studied the proportions to determine the width of the sleeves ruffle. This time they came out right. I finished around the bottom of the bodice with a ruffle of the pleated material.

The collar-type yoke was made as a collar that opened in the back and was fitted over to the neckline. The finished yoke has shoulder seams.

After cutting the yoke to resemble the picture, it was finished with a pleated ruffle around the outside edge. I then joined the bodice and the collar-type yoke at the neckline and finished the neck with a small lace collar. The lace was from a lovely handkerchief. Some of the lace covered her shoes.

The bodice and skirt were ready to be joined. Placing the bodice on the doll, I closed the back with pins. I then pinned the bodice to the skirt along the seam where the bodice and pleated ruffle had been joined, removed the entire dress from the doll, and hand sewed the seams where they were pinned, joining the bodice and skirt.

The back was finished with a placket and snaps. The veil is made from a rectangular piece of veiling folded to make two layers, with one layer longer than the other. The veil was gathered along the folded line and pulled to the desired size.

Scarlett's veil.

My version of Marlowe Cooper's creation.

My interpretation of the back.

I have dressed my version of the Bru June 13 in an exact copy of the 1800's style worn by the original dolls. Many French dollmakers commissioned expert dressmakers to design beautiful clothing for their porcelain dolls. Even the famous Worth, was known to create styles for dolls.

The original clothing I copied was shown on a Bru doll owned by Marlowe Cooper on page 27 of 'French Dolls' by Patricia Smith.

This beautiful dress looks difficult but is really very simple to make after you study and determine its construction.

Notice the skirt. There are two — one pleated and longer than the overskirt. The lace-trimmed second skirt consists of gathered pointed panels. The fact that the blouse hangs over the skirt at the waistline suggests an under-blouse or lining that supports the skirt and the jacket appears to be just that, a jacket which is separate from the dress.

The back has been left to my imagination. However, the drape of the sides of the jacket suggest tucks or pleats at the center back.

To make this costume, I first collected the material I wanted to use. The pink paleness of the

Karen Hansen's inter-relations.

A satin rose on the bonnet.

original didn't appeal to me and the Bru seemed to reject the paleness as well. Her beautiful eyes needed to be emphasized with a complimentary color, and I found it in a piece of fine brocade that went very well with the ivory satin I chose for the skirt. Using my method of pattern making and fitting, I made her underclothing in ivory-colored cotton trimmed with lace according to the style of the day.

I divided the picture into three equal sections, starting at the shoulders and ending at the shoe soles. So I would not harm the picture, I used black sewing thread stiffened with hair spray and laid it across the picture. I then measured the doll and divided that measurement into thirds, drawing the lines on a large piece of paper to equal the measurement taken on the doll.

Following the picture, a rough outline of the placement of the hemline, waistline, jacket length, sleeve length and length of the points on the overskirt can be drawn on the paper so you will know how long to make the skirt, the sleeve, the jacket, etc.

I first measured and fitted a sleeveless lining for the bodice lining and as a support for the skirt.

I stitched the side seams together (not the shoulder seams yet), and stitched the back seam, leaving an opening for putting the gown on the doll.

I realized part of the skirt was under the bodice blouse so, after determining the length plus additions, I cut the skirt double the length because I wanted the skirt double. I stitched the double skirt together along the raw edge side lengthwise, and pressed the skirt — especially the folded edge — after marking and pinning the pleats at the raw edge side. I stitched them with a machine stitch. Then I pinned the raw pleated edge to the ironing board, pinned the folded edge to match and pressed the pleats in.

I slipped the pins off the bottom just before the iron reached that area so the pin holes would not be pressed into the material. The pleated skirt was then sewn to the bodice lining with the seam on the right side. The overblouse will also be sewn to this seam, and the seam will be enclosed by the overblouse, making both sides of the garment neat.

After observing the picture, I

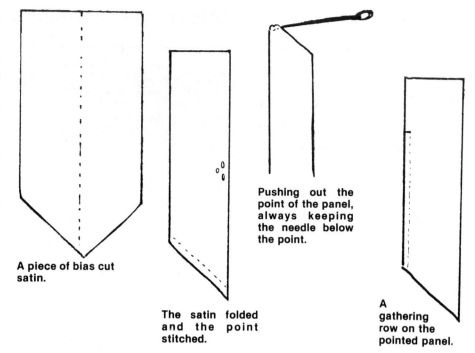

A piece of bias cut satin.

The satin folded and the point stitched.

Pushing out the point of the panel, always keeping the needle below the point.

A gathering row on the pointed panel.

decided to make eight panels for the overskirt. I divided the waist seam measurement into eight and added the seam measurement to each part to determine the width I needed to cut the panel. I also decided to cut them on the bias because the point would be on the straight and the gathers would be softer.

Rather than cutting a separate lining for the panels, I folded my material on the bias and pressed the fold. Then I cut the panels, making sure the points all turned the same way. The top of each

panel was cut on the square. I then turned them right sides together and stitched the short, straight side of the point.

They were turned and pressed, making sure the point was out completely. I have good luck getting the points out by using a needle. Place the point of the needle through the material at a distance along the seam below the point and push the point out. This takes several pushes and you need to place the needle point nearer the point each time.

Very often, when you try picking at it rather than pushing, you will pull out threads instead of the point.

The raw-edged side of the panel was gathered about ½ the way up from the bottom and the panels were stitched together. Because I cut the one side on the fold, I made the seam on the folded side very narrow. In fact, I just caught the very edge in the seam. The small amount of material gained by not taking a full seam was absorbed by the bias cut and didn't affect the fit at all.

After all panels were sewn to-

Marlowe Cooper's doll.

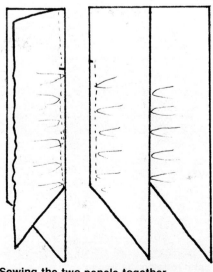

Sewing the two panels together.

gether, I hand stitched wide, gathered lace around the points, with extra fullness at the point ends and the lace ungathered at the point. The vee shape gave the lace the appearance of fullness.

The overskirt was basted to the pleated skirt at the waist seam. Using the bodice lining front pattern, I enlarged it for fullness and added two inches for the blouse hang-down. I didn't cut it all the way to the shoulder as there is a ruffle at the neckline in front. I allowed for the bodice overblouse piece to be folded over at the top for this ruffle.

The front section from the shoulder down to this ruffle is not gathered and is cut separately. I wanted added length and fullness at the bottom of the back bodice only so I split the lining pattern piece fan shaped and added the wanted length and fullness.

This portion of the dress was cut from a beautiful piece of knitted, patterned sheer that, because of fullness, was not see-through sheer and covered the waist seam very well.

After sewing the blouse side seams, I folded the front top under and machine stitched two rows of gathering across the top about ¾" down from the fold. I then sewed the gathered bottom of the blouse to the skirt at the waistline seam by laying the right side of the blouse over the right side of the skirt, matching the side seams and having the gathers even. When the blouse was turned up, the back pinned to the neck and shoulders and the front shoulder piece in place, I stitched the shoulder seams together and faced the neckline.

Next, the front piece was pinned and hand stitched in place with the front ruffle extended a little above the front finished neckline. The armholes were bound and the back of the garment was closed with a placket

Placement of the over-blouse for stitching.

and snaps.

The jacket pattern was made with a back piece and two front pieces that had enough material allowed on the bottom and sides to fold into tucks and reach the center back.

It's best to make a sample for this in muslin and, if your jacket material is very soft, the muslin can be used as an inner lining. After getting the pattern to fit as desired, cut the jacket in both material and lining.

I made the box-pleated trim around the jacket and sleeves of double self material cut the width way of the material because it folded better and pleated easier that way.

After sewing the back darts, shoulder seams and side seams on both the jacket and lining, I made my pleating with the measure and pleat method. That is, have a cardboard edge cut the size of each pleat and how much to fold under and, as I stitched, I would measure and slip the

material under the pressure foot and stitch again until I had the required amount of pleats.

With right side to right side I sewed the pleats all around the jacket from back seam to back seam. I then sewed the jacket and the lining together, clipped the seams and turned and pressed the edge, including the pleats.

In the picture the pleats were flat so I pressed mine down, but the pleated ruffle looked so nice without being pressed down that it gave me an idea for another dress.

After pinning the jacket and lining together at the armholes, I made the sleeves, sewed the pleated edge along the bottom and lined them by stitching the lining at the bottom to cover the seams. I then sewed the jacket part of the sleeve into the armhole and hand stitched the sleeve lining into the armhole, covering all of the seams.

A decorative braid was

stitched around the jacket at the pleated ruffle area. Finally I folded the tucks in the back through both the jacket and the lining and stitched them together. After opening the seam and hand catching the edges down flat, I brought the back bottom tucked part of the jacket up over the lower back bodice of the jacket. I tacked it in place with a beautiful rosette-type medallion made of rolled braid with two beautiful tassles made of fine silk cord that had formerly adorned an Oriental happy coat and was perfect for the jacket.

Her bonnet was made of the same material as the jacket and was trimmed to match. The satin-ribbon rosettes completed the outfit. In lieu of a Bru pin on the bodice, I substituted one of the pins that had been in our family for years. The shoes on my Bru are different from those in the picture as I wanted to experiment with a cloth shoe and I wanted them to match the jacket.

I like her well enough that I am planning to do her in a smaller version, about ½ the size, to see how the dress style adapts to the smaller scale.

May I sugest you use the following steps when copying a picture, and I can assure you that they will please you.

1. Study the picture to determine the construction.

2. Determine the material to be used.

3. Measure the picture and doll for proper proportions.

4. Plan how to do the unshown parts to blend with the shown parts.

5. Measure — cut and fit patterns, making them in muslin first if it is necessary to get the proper drape and correct lines before proceeding in the garment fabric.

Good luck with your project!

Chapter 13
Dressing Clowns and Other Characters

All clowns are not dressed in bright, colorful costumes using the one-piece, full-pajama like pattern. Some are more of a character doll than a regular circus clown, such as Charlie Chaplin - with his derby hat and cane.

In the early "reel" life of this actor/comedian, he wore the narrow pant leg of the era, but one day he put on the oversize, baggy pants of a fellow actor and liked the image they created. From then on he wore baggy pants.

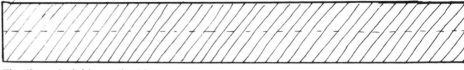

The tie material is on the bias.

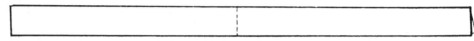

Fold the tie material lengthwise and mark the center.

Fold the tie at the center mark and cut where indicated.

Charlie.

The finished tie.

Hobo the clown.

I chose to dress my Charlie in the earlier version — the narrow leg — because I felt it gave him a more dapper look. If you choose the other style, increase the size, mostly through the upper legs and waist but increase only a little in the length. If you add fullness at the leg bottom, they will slip down over the shoes, especially if you have added too much to the length. So keep the leg bottoms narrow.

The instructions for his other clothing have been covered in the chapter on clothing for male dolls.

Our Hobo Clown is also reminiscent of another famous character who was a star of movies, circus and stage. In real life he presented a more tattered image with ragged clothing, but I preferred to use patches. Methods for constructing his clothing have been presented in previous chapters with the exception of his tie.

The tie is best if cut on the bias; it ties and hangs better and often the pattern in the material will be more interesting.

If your material, when on the bias, is not long enough, piece it together until you have a bias piece about 4" wide and as long as the measurement around his neck, plus 1½" for the knot, and twice the length desired to hang down from the knot. Now, press any seams open if you had to piece the tie material. Fold the material double lengthwise and again at the center of the folded piece. You now have four thicknesses.

The part of the tie that goes around the neck and forms the knot will be cut, through the four layers, 1" wide starting at the center fold. Then tapering cut the remainder of tie length out to the four corners (see diagrams).

If your tie is woven material and you have it on the bias, follow the grain of the material and cut a point.

Sew the tie, right sides in, together lengthwise, leaving both ends open. Turn right side out and press flat with the seam centered at the back side. Pull threads from both sides of the point to make a fringe and give the tie a frayed look.

For a tie without a frayed end, do not cut it to a point. But rather, after the tie is stitched and turned, fold the end to form a point and catch it by hand on the back side. If you wish, you can make one side of the tie narrow so that when the tie is on the doll the under part will be covered by the top side.

Hobo also has a red bandana handkerchief cut from a regular bandana. To finish the raw edges, I zig overcast them with black thread.

To complete his costume, I covered part of his hands with soft glove leather to give the effect of worn-out gloves. These are stitched on, by hand, and cannot be removed unless the stitches are cut.

His broom is made of straw, cut from my household broom, that has been wrapped around a wooden dowel and held in place with wire. I then pressed the straw part of the broom down into a pan of boiling water. This not only cleansed the broom, but also gave it a bent, used look as well.

As a general rule, the appeal of a Kewpie doll is the unclothed look, but my Kewpie, playing at being a clown, needed a costume for a complete look. So I hum-

The Kewpie doll.

My sweet Becky as a clown.

As a clown.

Becky with a friend.

ored her with a traditional clown outfit — just a simple suit, like the little romper suit, explained in the chapter on male doll clothing. Just add length and fullness, and add elastic at the wrist and ankles, with a drawstring at the neckline. Trim as desired.

Our large, 27" green-headed clown is a different matter altogether. The fact that I could see it in my mind's eye with a hoop around the middle presented a problem, so I attached straps to the hoop and hung it

over the doll's shoulders, letting it hang down to where I wanted it at the waist. I then measured from the shoulder over the hoop down to the ankle for the suit's length. I also measured around the hoop and allowed extra for fullness so I would know how wide to make the pattern.

I was surprised to find that the crotch needed to be very short, something I wouldn't have thought about if I hadn't put the hoop on the doll and measured. That is why I suggest, when dressing dolls, always put everything on the doll that goes under the finished garment before making the pattern and fitting the outer garment. It will eliminate mistakes.

I discovered on this clown that I couldn't use elastic around the wrist because to have the openings large enough to go over the hands and feet, they would be too large for the wrist and ankles. I solved that problem by using drawstrings. I could have used a band and placket, closing it with buttons or snaps, but the drawstring is easier, quicker and works very well. The string ends can be slipped up inside, between the ankle or wrist and the garment. The neck also closes with a drawstring. The ruffle is made separately to fit the neck.

Because the hoop I used was solid, I couldn't slip it through a casing. So, I machine stitched one side of the ½" casing on the waistline area, and hand stitched the other side, enclosing the hoop as I stitched. The top waist ruffle is tacked in several places over the hoop.

Cotton pompoms completed the outfit, even on the top of his store-bought hat.

Another thing about this outfit...I found the polka dot material I wanted to use in a soft knit only so I used a backing, or lining, or crinoline to give the soft

A beanie or skull cap for the wig base.

Sewing on the first row of braid.

Sewing on the second row of the braid after the first is folded down.

material body, and sewed the two materials as one.

If you are interested in making a wig such as the green one on this clown, use macrame yarn. I found a yarn that was woven in a braided pattern that unraveled without much effort. Proceed by making a loose skull cap for a base and stitching the short cut folded lengths of macrame cord to the cap through the center fold. Be sure to sew the cords close together in rows, having the cords touching each other. Make the rows about ½" apart.

Perhaps you will, as I did, think that you have too much wig; don't worry, you haven't, because if the cords are too far apart, the finished wig will have parts in it. Continue sewing cord until the entire cap is covered. You will discover the reason for originally fitting the cap closely, as the stitching has absorbed the excess fullness.

Now settle down to a good TV show and unravel all of the macrame strands down to the cap. (It may take two TV shows!)

Brush the wig with a wire brush and glue it to the doll's head. After the glue is dry, snip away and give the wig a haircut, first around the face and then trim all over the head if needed to give a rounded effect.

The lovable Katzenjammer Kids will be new to a great number of readers because they are "cartoon characters" from a bygone time, and it took research on my part to dress them authentically. Their names are Hans and Fritz, and they are 9" tall. The only thing about those two that hasn't been mentioned in other chapters is the pair of striped trousers. I was unable to find the material I wanted in the color or stripe needed so I made my own stripes on a piece of blue material with a black felt-tipped marker, using a ruler to get the lines straight.

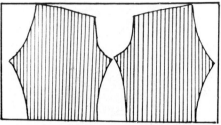

Stripes drawn on plain material with a felt tip pen.

I first traced the pant pattern on the material, then drew the stripes within the pattern area only, lining up the stripes so they would match when they were sewn together.

A felt-tipped marker can be used on other materials as well, but be sure to test first because the color has a tendency to run or spread on some fabrics.

This Oriental costume was patterned after an original which was displayed in a local Oriental cafe. The skirt is double with each skirt lined and made separately. The wide binding around the bottom of each skirt is folded over cotton padding to give them each a rounded look. The long cuff is also lined and left open in the back to serve as a pocket.

Her headpiece consists of a variety of items, glued together

An Oriental doll.

King Midas.

with craft glue. They were positioned on a cap made from gold paper doilies. I used several doilies together for firmness. It was necessary to prop some of the pieces to hold them in place while drying. I also had to use a generous amount of glue.

King Midas and his golden daughter were a joy to make. I thought about the idea for a long time until I had the total concept pictured in my mind. Then I gradually accumulated the required materials and fabrics, so that when I started the project everything was at hand.

This time, however, I did make a change from my original concept when I found that the piece of metallic brocade cloth I had planned to use for the King's cloak, along with the brown fur, didn't go well with the hair color on the doll I used for King Midas. So I substituted a plain-color velour and white fur, and was very pleased with the result. This can happen frequently. When you picture something in your mind and cannot find the exact material, very often what you substitute will look better; but picturing it in your mind will give you a basis from which to proceed.

The King has a cloth body made according to cloth bodies in Chapter 1, with one exception. I wanted to be able to position the arms on him, as well as the daughter, so I inserted wire in the arms. You can wire the arms so they are connected and one control the other or they can be made so they are independent and can be placed in any position desired.

Some coat hangers are made of wire that is quite heavy. This wire is fine for large dolls, but for King Midas I used a thinner wire found on a coat hanger that had wire arms inserted into a cardboard tube used by cleaners for hanging pants. I cut a length long enough to fit into the porcelain arm and up over the shoulder and top of the doll's body, a little past the center, so that the wires from each arm will overlap. Wrap the arm or hand end with masking tape and insert down as far as possible into the porcelain arm. Now proceed to finish the arm as previously instructed, keeping the wire in the center of the stuffed arm. Make the joints as usual, bend the wire over the shoulder and stitch the arm down. The wire will extend fur-

The golden Princess has a body of gold cloth.

ther than the cloth arm and, when both arms are in place, the wires should overlap through the center area. Whip stitch them together to the body.

The King is wearing gold pants, Ultra Suede boots and a blouse of iridescent brocade trimmed in gold braid. His cloak is lined with a complementing shade of velour and held together with three gold-headed pins. Lace, sprayed gold, fashions his crown, and the boots are laced

King Midas without his cape.

The velvet board. Note the hidden stands.

and tied with regular sewing thread of a deeper color.

The cape was sewn by hand with the two right sides together, and stitching the fur inside so only the hair part of the fur would show when the cape was turned right side out.

The collar was made the same way. Then the two were joined at the neckline and, as I mentioned before, closed with three gold-headed pins.

Our little "Golden Princess" is made of porcelain and painted with 22 carat gold which was polished with silver polish after firing. Her body is made of muslin covered with a fine, metallic-gold fabric. Her gold-lined skirt is trimmed with gold cord, sequins and braid.

The sleeves and bodice are a piece of sheer silk run through with gold metallic threads about 1/8" apart. Because I wanted the sleeves to stand out, I lined them with two layers of white tulle. The sheer bodice was lined with a piece of white taffeta.

Inasmuch as I wanted both dolls to be firm on their stands, and they were to be together on a board, I had the stand base screwed to the board. The board was to be covered with a piece of velvet. So I marked and cut two slits in the velvet that corresponded with the upright part of the stands, and slipped the velvet over the upright part of the stands down to the board, and thumb-tacked it to the board around the edges.

After King Midas was dressed, but before placing his cape, I put the body holding part of the stand around his waist, making sure it fit him firmly. The ends can be bent to achieve a snug fit. The two parts of the stand were then put together. After making sure he was exactly where I wanted him, I used a pair of pliers to pinch the two stand sections together so the doll would

Jackie in the box.

Hans...or

Fritz Katzenhammer

stay in place. I did the same with the daughter, by slipping the doll holding part of the stand under her dress and slip. This hid the stand and makes the overall appearance more attractive.

This project was truly a joy to plan and complete.

Another fun project was the large "Jackie" in the box. This doll has only one-half of a body with a round post holding up that half-body. The half-body is made of cloth stuffed with batting. She also has the post going through her body to the neck. If you move her left hand up and down, she will shake the jester. This was accomplished by wiring the arms with one piece of heavy clothes hanger wire, using the same method as for King Midas. This was a little more complicated because I also had the wire run through the upper part of the post. This project would be lovely as a music box.

The square dancers are a saucy pair and their clothing construction has been featured in another part of this book. However, note his designer jeans and how her full slip holds out her skirt.

I have a wonderfully gifted artist friend living in Utah, whose talents are in many fields. Her name is Diane Martindale,

Mother Hulda as Golda. Sculpted by Diane Martindale.

—85—

and I am proud to have some of her originals.

Her "Mother Hulda" reminded me of a former Prime Minister of Israel so I dressed her as I imagined she would have dressed to attend a formal function. Her underwear is conservative and handmade, and the water-wave silk in her skirt was a piece of wide ribbon I found among my mother's things after she was no longer alive.

Mr. and Mrs. Wong. Sculpted and dressed by Diane Martindale.

The gray silk organza blouse is shirred. This not only gives fullness and design, but controls the fit as well. The dainty lace collar and cuffs are part of the lace trim from a handkerchief.

I also own a wonderful pair of Chinese peasants sculpted and dressed by Diane. They are #13 in a limited, numbered edition and are an example of a simple straw hat triggering an idea. Diane purchased the hats, and Mr. and Mrs. Wong are what she put under them. The clothing is authentic and the jacket closures are wood, burned to resemble bamboo as are the hair sticks which hold her hair in place. The thongs are fashioned from leather, and their clothing is unisex.

Sioux War Chief. Sculpted and costumed by Judy Anderson. Notice the authentic bead work.

I am fascinated by what other doll artists do, and unusual dolls have a great deal of appeal to me. A doll in this category is a Sioux War Chief, one of a series of dolls depicting the everyday heroes of yesteryear, sculpted by Judy Anderson.

He has a porcelain head-shoulder plate and porcelain hands, with a jointed cloth body. His clothing is made entirely of buckskin and is trimmed with real beads on the war bonnet, war shirt, leggings and moccasins. The war bonnet and lance are made using pigeon feathers, hand-dyed to resemble eagle feathers. The shield is hand-painted.

Books on Indian lore and beadwork were used to learn about proper clothing construction and design motifs of the Sioux tribe.

The Indian Chief is authentic with a few liberties. Those differences are as follows:

The shield was made from buckskin rather than rawhide. To avoid a bulky appearance to the clothing, the fringe on the leggings and sleeves is on one side only. The breechclout is made in two pieces which attach to the belt that holds the leggings up, and the beading designs had to be adapted to utilize a smaller number of beads.

A truly magnificent doll.

Judy's husband Ed Anderson also sculpts and makes unusual dolls. His version of Henry the Eighth has an intriguing elf-like head and ears, with fascinating clothing designed and made by Ed himself.

These talented people and their dolls certainly inspire and challenge me. I hope that the information given in this book will inspire you to make your dreams come true.

Chapter 14

Odds and Ends

It seems that there are a few things left to talk about that haven't been covered in the preceding chapters. One is the wooden-arm pressing board that is so handy for pressing small seams open, especially collar corners and inseams on male doll trousers.

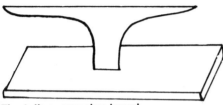

The tailors pressing board.

This board is made of two pieces of **hardwood** measuring 14"x6" and is ¾" thick. One board is the base and the other is cut to make the pressing arm. It actually has two arms, one at each end with one arm longer than the other. Lay the arm piece flat and draw an even line through the center. Measure and draw a line 1" from the top edge lengthwise. Make a mark on the second line 6" from the left end and another mark on the same line 4" in from the right edge.

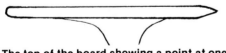

The top of the board showing a point at one end and a rounded end on the other.

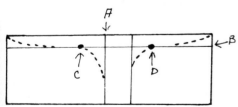

The diagram for cutting the upright section of the board.

Draw a perpendicular line, parallel to the first line, 5" in from the right side. Check the diagram for drawing the arms

and cut the board as illustrated. The top of the board is rounded on the long arm and pointed on the short arm, and both are tapered to the end. The cut area will need to have the edges rounded and sanded very smooth as the wood is not painted because of the heat of the iron.

The arm board is bolted to the base wth the ends of the arms even with the ends of the base and the arm board centered lengthwise. Strips of felt can be glued to the bottom of the base along the ends to protect the table or other surface. While on the subject of making pressing easier, I cannot say enough about using the iron or other pressing methods, such as a small light bulb, all through your sewing. It is difficult to press the tiny **completed** garment, especially the seams. A lighted Christmas light globe can press out puffs, ruffles and sleeves.

A soft cloth such as a man's white handkerchief makes an excellent pressing cloth. I usually remove the hem and wet and wring out one-half of the cloth. I then open the cloth flat and fold the dry area over the wet area and fold it in three, I then roll it tightly, then unroll and the entire cloth is the right dampness for pressing.

All materials do not need cloth pressing, but for those that do, a cloth will prevent shine and give a finished look to the pressing.

Often a lady doll will look unfinished and, as you study her, you realize she needs a purse or parasol or perhaps gloves. There are various styles of purses from the folded envelope style to the fancy beaded bag. Perhaps we can make a couple of styles in be-

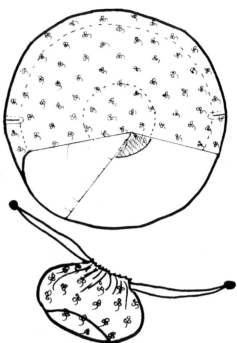

A simple lined drawstring purse with a rounded bottom.

tween those two.

A purse with a drawstring is fairly simple to make and can be very plain and practical or fancy and decorative. The basic pattern will serve for both, and what you do with material and trim will determine the finished product. You will need a circle large enough for a bottom, for sides and, in some styles, a hem or ruffles. Our basic purse will have neither a hem or a ruffle.

To make a plain purse, cut the circle in fabric and one in lining. Cut a small circle of cardboard or plastic. Plastic detergent, bleach, milk or other bottles are excellent for this purpose. Place it in the exact center of the fabric piece on the wrong side and, after putting the lining in place over it, stitch the two materials together around the plastic disc.

Divide the outside edge of the fabric in two and mark. Make a slit from the outside toward the center of the fabric, at each mark, long enough to accommodate a drawstring with ease, and bind the slits with a piece of self-bias material. Pin the outside edges of both the fabric and lining circles together and bind them with self fabric or ribbon. Stitch the two materials around the outside, leaving room between the outside binding and the stitching for the drawstring casing.

Cut two lengths of cord for drawstrings and thread one length through one opening all around and out the same opening. Do the same with the other cord, through the opposite opening. You will have two ends out one opening, and two ends out the other.

Make the ends equal in length, and tie the two ends at one opening together and the two ends at the other opening together. Now pull one knot with one hand and the other knot with the other hand and you will close the top of the purse or bag.

As you can see, this is very simple and basic and the possibilities for other purses are many. Try leaving extra material on the fabric part only for a ruffle, or sew a ruffle on the main part of the purse which will hang down as far as the bottom disc.

You could make it different by cutting the circle as small as the bottom and gathering or pleating a straight piece of fabric and sewing it to the circle. The top could be sewn into a band and drawstrings threaded through the band.

To give this style purse a plump look, make the lining just large enough to fit around the disc and shorter than the fabric. When the top of the lining and the longer top of the fabric are sewn together, the gathered fabric part of the purse will puff out.

This basic purse can be made small and beaded all over with bead fringe around the disc. There are so many possibilities, so let your imagination go and dream up some beauties.

A parasol can make an ensem-

An open parasol.

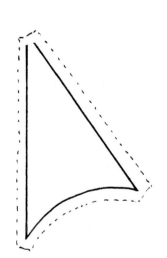

A pattern for the open parasol sections.

A fan, the sections can be cut from a plastic milk bottle. They can also be covered.

ble complete, and as parasols were designed for protecton from the sun only, they can be as fancy and pretty as we want to make . They will never see rain as that is left to the umbrella.

There are parasol frames on the market that are permanently open and some that open and close. Choose the one you want

and cover it to complement the doll's outfit. I find the best way to make the parasol covering, or main part, is to cut it in pie-shaped sections which fit between the parasol ribs.

Cut the material so that the widest part of the wedge will be on the straight of the material so it will not stretch. Stitch the

—88—

pieces together and place it on the frame for proper fit. Do not sew the fabric to the frame at this time, but remove it and sew the trim in place. All the decorations should be stitched on before stitching to the ribs, with the exception of the trim on the center of the parasol near the end of the parasol tip.

On a permanently open parasol with a wire handle, I straighten out the hook on the end of the handle, put glue on the wire and wrap cord around it close together so the cord lays in close rows. A wooden bead or any other object you wish can be attached to the end of the corded wire for a handle with a loop of cord to fit over the hand so the parasol will stay in place on the doll.

A beautiful closed parasol can be made with a dowel, a wooden bead and a circle of cloth that has been trimmed with lace, ruffles or whatever you wish. After decorating the circle, make six or eight creases on the inside of the parasol fabric. These creases should be evenly spaced. An easy way to make eight is to pretend you are cutting a pie into eight pieces by marking first in halves then quarters and then eighths. For six sections, use the same system. Be sure the creases are creased to the inside.

Slip the dowel down through the parasol through a small hole in the center of the circle and attach it to the dowel with a bit of glue. Let the glue dry so the parasol will not slip up the dowel while you are finishing it. Attach the parasol to the dowel on each crease, using glue and spacing the folds evenly. Add trim to the bottom of the parasol and dowel. Of course, you painted the dowel and wooden bead or ball the desired color first, didn't you?

A few tips about several things that I find make sewing easier . . . When stitching short amounts on

A parasol made by gluing fabric on a cone and attaching it to a dowel.

A circle of cloth gathered around a dowel.

the machine, do not cut the thread each time you come to the end of the piece; slip the next piece under the pressure foot and continue to sew. For example, sew one shoulder, and without doing anything, sew the next shoulder, then the side seams. Cut the shoulders apart and without ending or cutting the thread at the machine needle, slip the bodice under the foot and sew in a dart. Go on to another piece the same way and you will save time because the thread will not keep slipping out of the needle when you start to sew each time. If you need to make the ends of the seams secure, just

backstitch for a stitch or two.

When sewing tucks on a bodice or other short piece, I fold a small piece of material and sew onto it at the end of each tuck. I can then cut the bodice from the end of the small piece of material and sew another tuck without a lot of long threads. It takes practice to remember to slip the small piece of material in each time but I do recommend that you try it.

Another thing that I suggest is that you always wash your hands before starting to sew, especially hand sewing.

To pin-push gather and sew a ruffle to the bottom of a slip in one sewing, first divide and mark the ruffle and slip bottom into an equal number of sections. It's easy to use the side seams as marks and the center front and back as other marks, additional marks can be centered between these marks. It doesn't matter how many marks you have just as long as you have the same number on the ruffle as you have on the slip and they are evenly spaced. Pin the ruffle to the slip bottom at the marks and place the slip under the pressure foot and put the needle down through the material at one of the marks, push the ruffle material under the foot as you sew in little pleats with a pin, a sewing needle or a used sewing machine needle. This is a quick way to sew on a ruffle.

This method of sewing on ruffles does not give you as even looking a ruffle as the double thread method but does look alright on slips.

Ruching — that is short ruffles gathered through the middle — can be made by pushing the material through the pressure foot while sewing using both fingers of both hands.

I also suggest that you mark the grain line on the patterns so your patterns will all match and the garments cut from them will be on the same grain. Also draw arrows on the back of material with a nap for easier cutting.

If you need your scissors sharpened in a hurry try using a soda pop bottle. Simply open the scissors and hold the neck area of the bottle between the blades and move the blades in a cutting motion using pressure on the neck of the bottle neck. The blades may have a tendency to slide up and down on the neck but that doesn't matter.

Mittens and gloves are not used very often on dolls, but if you want to make them, here are some suggestions. Knitted or crocheted cap, scarf and mittens can be made for a medium to large size doll by using the small crochet hook or the tiny knitting needles, the one strand yarn and

a real baby-size pattern. They can also be made from knitted material or even socks or stockings.

Little lace half-gloves or mitts look nice with some lady doll costumes, and fingered leather gloves are a real challenge, requiring glove leather, glover's needles and the patience of Job. They also require a doll with separated fingers.

I've tried to cover each phase of dressing dolls and explaining as well as picturing many of the steps. The glossary may further inform you about some of the words used in the text.

In closing this book, I wish to suggest that if "my way" has helped you, please pass the word along and hopefully there will be other doll dressmakers who will find that dressing a doll beautifully can be a joy and give one a feeling of satisfaction.

Happy Doll Dressing,
Helen B. Hansen

A fan made of pleated paper and flat toothpicks.

Push gathering a ruffle with the fingers.

Ending your stitching on a piece of scrap material. If you wish you can secure the end of the ruffle stitching by back stitching.

The finished parasol.

This doily has been saturated with sugar water and attached to a pointed dowel by pushing the point through the center of the doily and standing it on a styrofoam half ball. The doily is then shaped and held to the dowel with thread until it is dry.

A quick way to sharpen scissors.

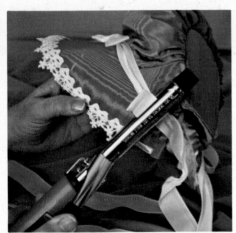

Pressing a flat bow with the iron, the setting is on hot.

The pressed loop.

Measuring the hem of a coat.

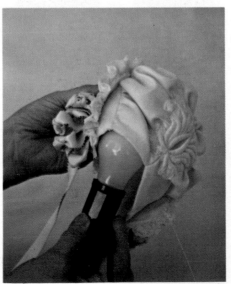

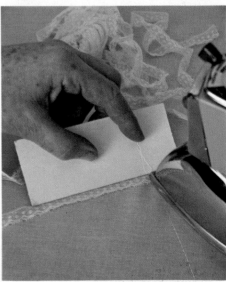

Removing lint from velvet with masking tape.

Pressing that hard to get at place with a light globe. Use a ten or five watt globe only. Large Christmas lights can also be used.

Holding narrow lace with a piece of cardboard for ease in pressing.